WHO'S YOUR
BARTENDER?

WHO'S YOUR BARTENDER?

The
Secret Techniques and Basics of Bartending

David Vancil

Order this book online at www.trafford.com
or email orders@trafford.com

Most Trafford titles are also available at major online book retailers.

Printed in the United States of America.

ISBN: 978-1-4269-6376-6 (sc)
ISBN: 978-1-4269-6377-3 (hc)
ISBN: 978-1-4269-6378-0 (e)

Library of Congress Control Number: 2011905491

Trafford rev. 01/27/2012

 www.trafford.com

North America & International
toll-free: 1 888 232 4444 (USA & Canada)
phone: 250 383 6864 ♦ fax: 812 355 4082

TABLE OF CONTENTS

Preface

This book is for beginners—the ones who aspire to be the "world's best bartender"; the ones who love it when their bartenders put their drinks on the bar—*boom*—before hitting them with a "hello" or a handshake. This book is dedicated to the next generation—no sifting through bar books written fifty years ago.

This book is also dedicated to all of the bartenders I have worked with. They, along with my customers, brought special things to me as a person and to this book. I thank you.

Why Be a Bartender?

WHY NOT?

You're the little guy until you pay your dues. You have to realize what you are getting into, but ....

As a bartender you make cash and connections and have unbelievably great times. You possess a skill—no expensive tools necessary. Such skill empowers you to travel to distant countries and work. You could open your own pub, bar, or nightclub. You could work in Las Vegas doing flair shows, in a swanky jazz bar in New York, a strip club in Chicago, a cabaret in Tokyo, a dance club in Waikiki, a little dive bar in Los Angeles, or a little beach bar in the Bahamas.

I have so many fond memories because of bartending! Countless times I've awakened from an unbelievable night and/or morning thinking, "I wonder what is going to happen today—blow jobs, birthday shots, body shots, and just plain craziness." Just when you think you've seen it all—why be a bartender?

You'll have to decide for yourself …

The Lingo

As is the case with any craft, in order for you to understand the rituals, signs, and symbols of bartending we need to break them down for you. In the beginning it may be hard to understand the words people are throwing at you. My first night behind the bar, I understood nothing as people asked for things "neat," "up," and "with a back"; there was even a request for "fire in the hole." At one point I dropped a bottle in the trash because my hands were wet, all the while being watched by bartenders, managers, and the owner. That wasn't the worst of it. It just so happened that the most beautiful creature in the world to me at the time was staring at me, waiting for me to get off work! Arggh! Things did not go as planned. Let's make sure you are better prepared!

Pourer: *measuring tool inserted into the tops of bottles. The pourer is designed to keep excited bartenders from pouring too much.*

Count Fast: *using a fast pourer, pouring and counting to one. Fast pourers are used for syrups and juices, except lemon juice, lime juice, and grenadine. 1 count = 1 oz.*

Count Slow: *using a slow pourer, pouring and counting to four. Slow pourers are used for liquors, cordials, lemon juice, lime juice, and grenadine. 4 counts = 1 oz.*

Jigger: *tool used to measure liquid. This tool is designed to teach you to execute a recipe without pinches, dashes, or splashes. Sizes vary.*

Counting and Bottle-Holding Tips

1. Always hold the neck of the bottle with your pinky, ring, and middle fingers while your index finger wraps on top of the pourer. This secures the pourer, making sure it will not pop out.

2. Always make sure the back end of the bottle is straight up when you're pouring.

3. Always curl the bottle to stop the flow of liquor, keeping the bottle close to the forearm. Never let the bottle drop down so that it crashes into other bottles and breaks while you are pouring.

4. Practice with a bottle full of water, three glasses, and a shot glass/jigger. Make sure your four counts are always the same. After you pour into the glasses check the level on all of them and then pour the water from the glass back into the jigger to make sure the amount you poured was "right on the money," not under or over. If you can't get your four count to pour consistently, then you should practice more before you free pour.

How Much Is Too Much…?

A Shot = *1 oz.*
On the rocks—*on ice with eight counts, topped with ice again; that's right*—2 *oz.*
Chilled—*put on ice in a tin/shaker, shake, and pour*
Dash/pinch—*1 tsp.*
Splash—*¼ oz. (1 count)*

Who Starts a Party
LIKE "Martinis" Start a Party!

The Martini is one of the hottest drinks of the century.
A splash of Vermouth in a martini
was popular during the 1920s.
Today, the drink is often sent back
because of too much vermouth.

VERMOUTH
Just Don't Do It!

Shaken or Stirred . . .
Dry—light on the vermouth, from a splash to none at all
Perfect—with sweet and dry vermouth

Are You Straight, Neat, or Naked . . .?
Straight up—*liquor served in a glass with a*
stem; for example, a martini/cocktail glass
Up—*liquor served in a glass with no stem; for*
example, a shot glass
Straight/Neat/Naked—*liquor served in a glass*
with no stem and no ice at room temp;
for example, Scotch neat = Scotch with no ice in
a small bucket

*   *   *

Wine the Cooler Way ...
Spritzer—3 oz. (3 counts) of wine on ice with a splash of soda
Cooler—3 oz. (3 counts) of wine on ice with a splash of Sprite

Staying on "Top" and Mixing It Up ...

Float—*to place one type of liquor on top of another, or on top of a drink; 1 oz. = 4 counts*
Layering—*floating one liquor or cordial on top of another*
Muddling—*crushing or grinding herbs with a muddler (stick)*

Having a Ball ... a Highball

Highball—*1 oz. liquor and Sprite*
Press or Presbyterian—*1 oz. liquor, soda, and a splash of ginger ale*
Back—*a small rocks glass full of ice and a drink; for example, Coke*
Buck—*1 oz. (4 counts) liquor, 2 oz. (8 counts) lemon, and ginger ale; for example, gin buck*
Sour—*1 oz. (4 counts) liquor, 3 oz. (3 counts) (fast pourer) sweet and sour*

Getting Fizzy With It ...

Collins—*1 oz. liquor, 3 oz. (3 counts) of sweet and sour, and soda*
Rickey—*1 oz. liquor, 3 oz. (3 counts) of lime juice, and soda*
Fizz—*1 oz. liquor, 3 oz. (3 counts) of sweet and sour, and soda (Egg whites optional in a fizz)*

Priceless Information

1. Simple sugar=sugar syrup=gum syrup

2. Sweet and sour: lemon juice, simple sugar, and water

3. Orgeat syrup: almond-flavored simple sugar

4. Ginger ale can be made with Sprite and a splash of Coke (a couple of dashes of bitters are optional).

5. Bourbon is made in Bourbon County in Kentucky. Anything else is just whiskey.

6. Liquor: a distilled alcoholic beverage. Wine and beer are fermented.

7. Liqueur: flavored and/or sweetened alcoholic beverages

8. Cordials: alcoholic beverages that originally had a tonic or stimulating medicinal affect

9. Aperitif: alcoholic drink taken before a meal to stimulate the appetite

10. Digestif: a drink consumed at the end of a meal usually to aid in digestion, sooth the stomach, or in the case of higher alcohol content, to burn a hole to make room for more!!!

Big Bartenders' Tools

Jigger: The measuring tool no one uses, except perhaps in hotels and by bartenders-in-training.

Pourer: A measuring tool attached to a bottle top that controls the flow speed of the liquid.

Two types of pourers exist, a slow pourer and a fast pourer.
1. *A slow pourer* pours liquor, lemon and lime juice, and grenadine.
2. *A fast pourer* pours fruit juices (except lemon and lime), sugar syrup, sweet and sour, and milk.

Shaker/Tin: A container used to soften the taste of liquor by chilling it. It's a cool place where your ice and liquor hang out. The shaker is used to chill and shake liquor and cocktails, scoop ice, and open bottles.

Glass Tumbler: Either a glass that may be used on top of the shaker or another smaller shaker.

Strainer: Used to filter ice out of the shaken liquor, cocktail, or shot. Another smaller shaker may also be used.

Stirrer/Spoon: A metal tool for mixing the cocktail. The stirrer/spoon can be used to evenly distribute the liquors without interfering with the harmony of the other liquors in a shot or layered drink. A straw could be used to stir a cocktail as well.

AND OF COURSE A ...

Lighter: For the ladies—and the other customers too. As a working bartender, you should always have two things in your pocket: a lighter and a wine key. At a moment's notice, light the customers' cigarettes and don't be a lazy bartender. And keep the ashtrays clean—all that is needed is a paper napkin and a half second to clean the ashtrays. Always remember that the bar is a reflection of you! How clean is your bar?

Bottle Opener/Wine Key: This one is self-explanatory. Choose a good one!

A Nice Piece of... GLASS

Hurricane 15 oz.　Daiquiri 10.5 oz.

Old Fashion/
Rocks/Bucket
10 oz.

Highball/Collins
9 oz.

Snifter/Brandy
6 oz.

Champagne/
Flute 6 oz.

Wine 6.5 oz.

Martini 5 oz.

Margarita 7 oz.　Beer mug 10 oz.　Coffee 8 oz.

Tequila Shooter
1.5 oz.

Pilsner 10 oz.　Shot 1 oz,　Pony 1.5 oz

Protect Your Temple;
Don't Cut Your Hands

- Always clean lipstick off glassware with a napkin or a rag.
- Always hold glassware by the base while washing it, and avoid getting cut by broken glass.
- Always use a napkin/cloth to polish the wine glasses. One napkin-covered hand holds the base and the other covered hand cleans the rim.
- Always use paper napkins to wipe a sink out that had a broken glass in it.
- Never use your bare hands!

How They Move So Fast

Set up drinks and knock 'em out—FAST!!!

Nice And Easy!!!

*G*rab the glasses you need as you listen to the customers' order(s) and/or read the ticket.

Set em' up! Follow the system and set up: 1) glasses; 2) blenders; 3) shakers; 4) shot glasses; 5) wine glasses; and 6) beer—in that order.

DO'S	DON'TS
Do everything you can without moving your feet. For example, if beer is in a cooler at the other end of the bar, make the drinks first and then go get the beer. Or if your glasses are iced and set up, get your beer before you start making drinks; then come back to the memorized glass setup. Every bar has a unique setup system, with both efficient and inefficient ways to do things.	Don't put the bottle down until you've used the required liquor in every drink. If you're making a tequila sunrise and blending a margarita you pick up the tequila (4 counts) and triple sec (2 counts), put down the triple sec, and then pour tequila in the tequila sunrise (4 counts). Next, you pick up the lime in your left hand (2 counts) and the grenadine in your right hand (2 count) and pick up the sweet and sour mix with your left hand (3 counts) and the orange juice with your right hand (3 counts).
Do use energy efficiently. Don't waste energy by walking back and forth; before you move, think about everything you will need. How many movements/steps are you making?	Don't pass objects from one hand to the other hand. If you pick it up with the right hand, then you should pour with the same hand. As a bartender, your hands are usually wet, and so the chances of your dropping a bottle are high. After you learn the system, you'll be ready to flip and throw bottles. Take baby steps!
Do practice using both hands. A good bartender should be ambidextrous. Before you know it, you're going to be opening bottles and doors with all types of body parts.	Don't step backwards. Finish whatever task you're on, with no hesitation!
Do prepare! Prepare! Prepare! Good bartenders prepare for customers, coworkers, and most importantly, themselves. A great bartender uses "the system" and checks the work afterwards as well as checking the work done by others.	Don't use excessive body movements. Did you move your feet two times unnecessarily when reaching for that bottle? Don't repeat yourself and move the liquor bottle twice. Get rid of excess body movements—quickly. Tip: Pick up your soda gun last and only once. Save time and don't develop bad habits.

DO'S	DON'TS
Do work left to right or right to left. Always work your way left to right or right to left, with your hands uncrossed, and always wash everything, returning it to where you found it. Flow ... work with and not against your environment.	Don't run around like a headless chicken. Set up, take orders, make drinks, or clean, and be sure to start from one end of the bar and work your way back, in circles! "Be like water." This is especially helpful when you're tired and your mental sparks aren't flying like they did at the beginning of your shift.
Do use both hands when making drinks; there's nothing busier than a one-legged man in an ass-kicking contest!	Don't be a one-handed Jack. Pick up three bottles at a time in each hand instead of one bottle. This saves time when restocking beer and wine bottles. Also, after cleaning bottles, use the same handgrip to return bottles to the rack after you've wiped them down. This handgrip is also useful for handling glassware.
Do calculate the total tab as you're making drinks. Give the total tab (verbally) to the customers before they receive any drinks, and then make change for the customer. If you're picking up money from two different customers, notice which hand each customer's money is in and return it to the right customer.	Don't forget what money the customer gave you. Repeat out loud the money you are changing: "twenty out of one hundred." Mistakes are expensive.

When the "Shit" Hits the Fan ... The System That Always Works

Everyone has seen a bartender moving around the bar like an octopus, helping small herds of people seemingly effortlessly, and all the while smiling! We don't spit in the eyes of tension and stress; we slide and dance like bamboo bending with the wind ... Okay, sometimes we step on toes, but all the while we smile!

When the "shit hits the fan," you should be able to fall back on *the system* and get you back into your groove. The system is a way to stay on top of things and involves four steps: 1) set up; 2) pouring; 3) building; and 4) executing.

1. *Set up* an order: put your glasses in place while the customer is ordering.
   - **Tip**—Keep glasses *rim to rim*. Don't waste the good stuff!

   - **Tip**—*Ice 'em up!* When building drinks, always go from left to right or right to left and never cross your hands. Whether working ice, liquor, or putting in the straws, always work left to right or right to left in circles, and keep your feet planted in one place.

   - **Tip**—*Ice 'em again!* (time permitting) No one wants a warm drink. Ice keeps the house happy (and costs down), and the customers keep coming back.

2. *Pouring* an order: Memorize and pour these liquors in the following order. If you forget everything else, remember this tip.
   - ➢ **R**ye
   - ➢ **B**ourbon
   - ➢ **B**randy
   - ➢ **S**cotch
   - ➢ **V**odka
   - ➢ **G**in
   - ➢ **R**um
   - ➢ **T**equila
   - ➢ **T**riple **S**ec
   - ➢ **C**ordials
   - ➢ **S**hots
   - ➢ **W**ine
   - ➢ **B**eer
   - ➢ **N**on-Alcoholic
   - ➢ **J**uices
   - ➢ **S**odas
   - ➢ **W**ater

Some bars will vary on the order in which they set up their bottles, but you should be able to adjust.

3. *Building your drinks* (still left to right/right to left)
   - ➢ Set 'em up
   - ➢ Ice 'em up
   - ➢ Liquor 'em up
   - ➢ Juice 'em up
   - ➢ Shot 'em up (using the soda gun). *In that order.*

   - • *Glass, Ice, Liquor, Juice, Soda.* How are you going to remember this one? Just say "*glass, ice, liquor, juice, soda*" every time you make a drink. You'll remember it.

4. *Executing* an order
   ➤ — *First:* build your drinks
   ➤ — *Second:* blend your drinks
   ➤ — *Third:* prepare your shots (these need tender loving care to make them "look purdy")
   ➤ — *Fourth:* empty your blender(s)
   ➤ — *Fifth:* shake and empty your shakers
   ➤ — *Sixth:* pop your beers

A BARTENDER'S MOTION STABBING AND JABBING

Pouring

Pour with a downward stabbing thrust. This motion will momentarily stop the flow of the liquor long enough for you to move to/jump to the next glass and never spill a drop.

How To:
Examples of Pouring

THE MORE DRINKS YOU POUR, THE MORE $$$ YOU MAKE!

Making multiple drinks at one time is a skill that comes with practice. Start with two-drink combinations and apply the system.

The System—Apply It!!!

Glass, Ice, Liquor, Juice, Soda
&
Rye, Bourbon, Brandy, Scotch, Vodka, Gin, Rum, Tequila, Triple Sec, Cordials, Shots, Wine, Beer, Non-Alcoholic, Juices, Sodas, and Water.

A vodka tonic and gin tonic

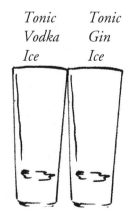

Tonic	*Tonic*
Vodka	*Gin*
Ice	*Ice*

Glasses touching   **Ice**   **Vodka**   **Gin**

1. Stand in the middle of the well and for every bottle to your right leg coordinate and use your right hand, and vice versa—any bottle to your left leg is handled with your left hand.

Once you pick up an item, always use *the same hand* for all functions before putting any item down. For example, when you pick up the soda gun for tonic, shoot the tonic into the vodka glass and gin glass and then put down the gun.

A vodka tonic, apple martini, and a rum and Coke

Tonic
Vodka
Ice

Apple pucker
Vodka
Ice

Coke
Rum
Ice

Coke
Ice

A Scotch with a Coke back, screwdriver, piña colada, and water

2. Never cross your hands.
3. Right and left hands are always moving at the same time.

While shooting the soda gun, garnish your drinks simultaneously.

Layering Chart

Start with your heavier ingredients firsts—the higher number, the heavier the ingredients. Pour using the back of the spoon. With a slow steady pair of hands you can also layer by pouring against the inside of the glass. Go slowly!! If you mix it up, let the drink stand for a moment. The ingredients should go to their designated areas.

For example…

LIQUOR/LIQUID	PROOF	COLOR
Southern Comfort	0.97	Light amber
Tuaca	0.98	amber
Water	1.00	White/Clear
en Chartreuse	1.01	green
Cointreau	1.04	white
Peach Liqueur	1.04	dark amber
sloe gin	1.04	white

*SEE APPENDIX FOR COMPLETE LISTING OF LAYERING CHART

DO'S BEHIND THE BAR	DON'TS BEHIND THE BAR
Do remember that the customer is always right!	Don't forget your tools— a lighter, gum, and a bottle opener/wine key.
Do remember—if it's worth doing, it's worth doing well.	Don't sleep with customers or people you work with; you can always run to your friends' bars and do that.
Do remember that once you're in the bar it's "show time." Good energy has everything to do with the customers' experience.	Don't bring any bad energy to work; leave it at the door.
Do make friends with the people you work with. Bars become like families; it's not just a job—it's a lifestyle!	Don't raise your voice or swear at a customer; if you do, you've lost. Remember that you're smarter and it's your bar.
Do keep your bar clean—you just never know ... and "if you have time to lean around you have time to clean around."	Don't drink too much! Bartenders have many things they are responsible for, so drink only in moderation. You want to be able to remember the good times!
Do keep your body clean—you just never know ... fingernails trimmed, showered, deodorant applied, etc. [Note: some employees need to be reminded!]	Don't forget that you're not indispensable.

DO'S BEHIND THE BAR	DON'TS BEHIND THE BAR
Do remember to always put back objects exactly where you found them.

Do teach others when there is an opportunity for you to move up and not out!

Do incorporate teamwork. One bartender mixes drinks while the other bartender makes change.

Do use good communication. Communication is important as you don't want one bartender starting a problem with the customer and trying to collect money that was already collected: "I got the money from ..." Also, communicate who's doing what: "I've got the piña colada ..." | Don't teach/train other coworkers when the opportunity is not there for you to move up.

Don't waste time. Time is precious; your words should be "short and sweet." Use "behind" for when you're behind coworkers and "slide" for when you need someone to move. It's not verbal, but placing your hand on the small of someone's back also helps to let people know where you are in the bar. Any lower than the small of the back is not recommended!

Don't let customers interrupt you. Only remember so many orders at a time. When you're ready then ask them what they would like. When your head is full of orders don't even open your mouth. It will throw you off and make you forget what you had in your short-term memory. Use body language if necessary. Use a little tact on this one. |

DO'S BEHIND THE BAR	DON'TS BEHIND THE BAR
Do always be aware. Know what's happening in your bar at all times. If the other bartender is making mai tais and your customer asked for one, ask him to make one more. If an ashtray is overflowing, empty it. If customers are finished drinking, clean up their glassware and help make room for the next customers to sit down.	Don't waste time when you are just too busy: "Sorry, the blender is broken," or "Sorry, we've run out of ..." "I'm sorry, I'd like to make that for you, but we don't have ..." I'm personally never too busy to make a blended drink. If you're good enough and have the right equipment it shouldn't take you that much more time. In a jam you can always make a bunch of the most popular drinks and just start asking who would like one.
Do use good questions before you make the drinks. "Vodka or gin?" "Absolute, Kettle One, or Grey Goose?" "Seagram's, Beefeater or Tangeray?" "On the rocks or straight up?" "Olive or a twist?" "On the rocks or blended?" "Salt or no salt?" "Will that be cash or credit?"	Don't treat your customers like they are only "$" signs. If you can't remember their names, remember their drinks; then make their drinks before they walk up to the bar!
Do recommend something. Ask customers, "Can I make you something nice?" This saves time and money.	

DO'S BEHIND THE BAR	DON'TS BEHIND THE BAR
Do say the most expensive item last when you're recommending liquor brands or wines. They're not listening to you anyway! They're checking out the girl next to them, looking at the bartender's big nose, thinking how expensive this place is … They'll choose the last choice you gave them because it's the only one they remember.	Don't just stand there; help customers make up their minds or disappear and let them ponder. You can ask them, "Wine, beer, or a cocktail?" After they have made a choice break it down for them: "White or red; Bud, Heineken, or Corona?" Nine times out of ten, given three choices, they will choose the last choice. Go ahead and grab the last suggestion, but don't show it to them. They will think that you're trying to push that one on them.

Remember
The Hair of the dog that Bit Ya ...

This is the only part of bartending that seems like school, without the naughty teacher in black-rimmed glasses, hair up, jacket, skirt, and black nylons; but don't think about it that way. Most drinks were created by someone in the midst of some crazy party while everyone was having a great time!

Think about where the cocktail was first created, imagine the ambiance and setting in which it was created, and feel the pride the bartender would have felt as people started to tell their friends about the incredible new concoction ... Use every sense you have to help you remember. *Read, write, imagine, touch, listen, smell, taste* [whatever it takes].

1. **Read** the recipe.

2. **Write** the recipe on a flash card.

3. **Imagine** yourself picking up the bottles and making the drink.

4. **Touch** the bottles, juices, and sodas [in the exact order] needed to create the drink.

5. **Listen,** actually hearing the pouring liquid, the air burping out of the pourer. "Blurb. Blurb. Blurb. Blurb … 1 … 2 … 3 … 4." The pouring of liquid and the actual gun have a distinctive sound.

6. **Smell,** using your sense of smell right before you taste the drink. Train your nose—is it sweet, sour, bitter, or spicy?

7. **Taste**—the one test you've been waiting for, just one quick sip with a straw or spoon. You want to train your tongue and question yourself: how do the combination of liquors and juices taste? Strong/sweet/sour? Balanced? Can you tell what is in a drink just by tasting it?

Take Baby Steps and know your stuff!

Knowing Your Stuff

Learn one recipe at a time without spending too much time on it.

Timing

Work in fifteen-minute intervals work with short breaks in between.

Reviewing Your Drinks

If you're not making all of the drinks you
learned every day, you'll forget them.
Remember the drinks that build on each
other or that are similar first.

Reminders

1. Leave the drink recipes all over the house on flash cards or Post-it notes so that you'll see and memorize them over and over. Keep copies on the refrigerator, on the wall across from the toilet, and on your car's visor to check while you are stopped in traffic.

The Random Quack

2. Randomly ask your friends if *they* know what's in a drink, but look the recipes up afterwards. Be careful, as everyone is an expert!

-IMAGINE/VISUALIZE-

How does a vacation in Hawaii sound?
Warm sand between your toes, the sound of the crashing
waves, drinking an ice-cold mai tai with light and dark rum
and fresh pineapple juice dripping down your chin as you
crunch into your pineapple garnish.

IMAGERY AND IMAGINATION are important when you're trying to remember drinks. Close your eyes and imagine yourself working the bar; see yourself going through all the steps of building that drink, from grabbing the glass to pouring the liquor and juice. Start this by having a map of all the bottles, beers, juices, and sodas—know the location of everything in the bar that you're working with. Know your bar well enough to be able to grab things without looking. Could you be blindfolded in this bar/your house and still make drinks?

Don't think of a Vodka & Fresh Squeezed O.J. as a SCREWDRIVER. Screwdrive Stuck in Your Head?

1 Imagine the recipe in a way that will help you remember the recipe. I remember a Harvey Wallbanger by envisioning a man with a bottle of vodka in one hand, Galliano in the other, and his private member stuck in a wall that is really a large orange.

> ➢ Harvey Wallbanger = 1 oz. vodka (4 counts), 3 counts of orange juice, and a float of Galliano (4 counts)

2. I remember a kamikaze with a vision of a Japanese pilot with a bottle of vodka in one hand, triple sec in the other, and a lime slice in his mouth, with his eyes bloodshot and determined. I even hear the noise of the plane going down. The more vivid the image the quicker you're going to remember.

> ➢ Kamikaze = 1 oz. vodka (4 counts), ½ oz. triple sec (2 counts), and 2 counts of lime

3. Tempt customers with drinks that they have never heard of or ones that you've just learned. This helps you remember the ones that aren't ordered often.

4 Silly Acronyms
For example:
Kamikaze
1½ oz. Vodka
½ oz. Triple sec
½ oz. Lime juice
= Very Tragic Landing
Or if you have an
Orgasm
½ oz. Bailey's
½ oz. Kahlua
½ oz. Amaretto
Splash of cream
= You might **Be Kind All** day? Whatever works for you …

WHat the **** Is That???

If you and your customer don't know what's in a drink, start with asking the basic questions, like what color it is and how it tasted.

When in doubt, make it red and put vodka in it … and smile!

Where does the name sound like it's from? If the drink has a tropical origin and you're debating between pineapple and orange juice—go with the pineapple juice ... Aloha!!!

If it's Italian ... Amaretto?
If it's Irish ... Baileys? Irish whiskey?
If it's Mexican ... Tequila? Maybe even a worm!
If it's slow ... Sloe Gin?
If it's crazy or screaming ... Vodka?

Stocking the Bar

Keep It Simple

1. Decide what beers, liquors, and wines you need; you can always add more drinks later.
2. Fill your freezers with juices, back-up juices (juices put into bottles), chilled liquors, chilled wines, Champagnes, bottled water, milk, whipped cream, garnishes, and chilled glasses.

WHAT TO STOCK

White Wine (1 of each)	Red Wine (1 of each)	Beer (2 of each)
Pinot Grigio	Pinot Noir	Domestic Beer
Chardonnay	Chianti	Light Beer
White Zinfandel	Merlot	Imported Beer
Champagne	Cabernet	Micro-Brews
	Syrah	
	Red Zinfandel	

2. Find a place for all your liquors and cordials and try to keep the bottles as close to the bartenders' well as possible.
3. Find a space for your condiments.

A Nice Balance

➤ *A large on-stock inventory:* three or four bottles of the well, call, and top-shelf liquors

➤ *A medium on-stock inventory:* two or three bottles of the well, call, and top-shelf liquors

➤ *A small on-stock inventory:* one or two bottles of the well, call, and top-shelf liquors

Have a set number and place for things.
The bar should be stocked and ready to go for the next shift when your shift ends.

THINGS TO KEEP IN MIND
WHEN STOCKING AND SETTING UP A BAR

Ask yourself these questions:

- Who are your customers?

- Why do they come to your bar—for entertainment, for food, or for you? When stocking any bar you need to begin by thinking about who your customers are going to be.

- Productive and efficient bars are stocked with a large supply of a few products.
- Provocative bars are stocked with hot chicks mixed with lots of liquor and good times.

**See back of book for sample inventory list.

Preparing for the Storm
and
Getting Ready for the Spanking

You know those days when you wake up late and in a hurry and you find out that there are only cheerios left to eat and realize that there's no milk—only after you've already poured the cheerios? You leave the house and forgot your phone. You miss the bus and have to pay for a taxi. You step out of the taxi and sure as **** you've stepped in it, and here comes the rain to piss all over you. Some people like this type of exhilaration. I like to be prepared. So that life doesn't CATCH you with your pants down, here are some outlines to keep you on track in the bar.

Basic Preparation
When you arrive ...

1. Turn on all your lights; then turn on the Co2 and check the CO2 level.

2. Put in a new garbage bag.

3. Run new hot soapy water in the sink.

4. Wipe down the bar.

5. Set up the wells with towels, mats, shakers, strainers, straws, napkins, pourers, beers, partial juices, and condiments.

6. Ice everything.

7. Get your money in order.

8. Prepare your lemons and limes, back-up juices, and wines. (Wine prep. is extracting the cork three-quarters of the way out without opening the bottle.)

9. Check for dirty and broken glassware and take care of it accordingly.

10. Review the checklist from the night before. If one wasn't made, make one of everything the bar needs and take care of it accordingly.

Cutting Fruit

Cut off the nipples first so that the fruit will stand upright. Always cut fruit by slicing forwards or backwards—*never* use force. If the blade is dull, use a different knife!

Basic Cleanup
When you leave ...

1. Soak your mats.
2. Melt—"burn"—the ice in the wells, but remember to save some ice.
3. Wipe down the countertops.
4. Pull out pourers and soak them in soda water while you clean.
5. Return the bottle caps to the bottle tops.
6. Empty your dirty water and put the mats somewhere to dry. Not dry = always wet = nasty bacteria.
7. Fill your sinks again with clean water and finish cleaning your glasses.
8. Pull out the bottles, wipe them down, and set them on the countertop. Make sure the countertop is clean and dry.
9. Return your glasses to their places and empty your sinks.
10. Wipe the wells and racks dry.

11. Return the bottles to the wells and racks.
12. Cover the bottles with plastic.
13. Start from one end of the bar and wipe the entire back of the bar down.
14. Start from one end of the bar and wipe the entire bar counter down.
15. Remove the pourers from the soda water.
16. With the used empty bottles, which are collectively called "the break", make a list of liquor needed for the next day. This is a good time to also write down what other things you need.
17. Restock what can be restocked. Leave the bar stocked the way you would like to have it stocked when you come in.
18. Set the trash outside the bar in order to take out on your way out.
19. Have yourself a beer and turn off the CO2.
20. Turn out the lights and take the trash out on your way out.

INTRODUCTION
TO
THE SECRET SAUCE
COCKTAIL RECIPES

It's a wonderful feeling when someone truly enjoys something you've made; especially when it's a cocktail that you've mixed and the first sip brightens their whole face. Any monkey can pour a beer, but only a great bartender can turn a beer into a Redeye, a Depth Charge, or a Flaming Dr. Pepper! Having a passion for eating and drinking translates into passionate cocktails, and people can taste it! The heart of a great cocktail has passion in it.

On the following pages you'll find recipes that most bartenders grew up with and old cocktail recipes that have been updated. The newest, most commonly made cocktails are at your disposal to create whether you're a bartender or are just hosting a party. I've researched each recipe and questioned every "Oh' wise one" I could find about these wonderful cocktails. About the cocktails' true origins and metamorphosis. Cocktails that were once popular become less so over time. This is because of the creation of new fashionable liquors. Trends change what liquors are fashionable; with those changes cocktails' base liquors change, leaving only the cocktails' name. The availability of various liquors and juices changes based on location. As bartenders travel, drinks are remembered, forgotten, and half-remembered. The half-remembered cocktails are not in this book. The book is intended to be a reference or "benchmark" so we, as bartenders, can all be on the same page.

Have fun with these recipes and remember the ones that you like and pass them on to a friend. Since everything runs in full circles, before you know it, somebody will be serving you a tasty cocktail!

RYE

RYE	RYE "DOES A BODY GOOD?"
WASHINGTON APPLE MARTINI	**RED SNAPPER BUCKET**
1 oz. Crown Royal (4 counts)	¾ oz. Crown Royal (3 counts)
1 oz. Apple Pucker (4 counts)	¾ oz. peach schnapps (3 counts)
2 oz. cranberry juice (2 counts)	1 oz. cranberry juice (1 count)

BOURBON	BOURBON ... EVEN THE WORD SOUNDS MEAN. WATCH OUT!
HOT TODDY-COFFEE GLASS 2 oz. bourbon (8 counts) 1 tsp. honey 1 oz. fresh-squeezed lemon 1 cup hot water	**LYNCHBURG LEMONADE HIGHBALL** 1 oz. bourbon (4 counts) ½ oz. triple sec (2 counts) 3 oz. sweet and sour (3 counts)
MANHATTAN-MARTINI 2 oz. bourbon (8 counts) 1 oz. sweet vermouth (4 counts) dash of bitters (optional)	**MINT JULEP-HIGHBALL** 2 oz. bourbon (8 counts) 2–3 sprigs of mint dash of sugar 1 oz. soda water (1 count)
OLD FASHION-BUCKET 2 oz. bourbon (8 counts) pinch of sugar 2 dashes of bitters splash of soda water cherry juice 1 orange slice, muddled an orange and a cherry for garnish	**THREE WISE MEN-BUCKET** 1 oz. Jack Daniels (4 counts) 1 oz. Jim Bean (4 counts) 1 oz. Johnny Walker Black Label (4 counts)
GORILLA FART-BUCKET 1 oz. 151 rum (4 counts) 1 oz. Wild Turkey (4 counts)	

BRANDY	OH, BRANDY ...!
B&B-SNIFTER 1 oz. brandy (4 counts) 1 oz. Benedictine (4 counts)	**BRANDY ALEXANDER-DAIQUIRI** 1 oz. brandy (4 counts) ½ oz. crème de cacao (dark) (2 counts) 3 oz. milk (3 counts), blended or served up topped with nutmeg
SIDE CAR-MARTINI-SUGARED RIM 1 oz. brandy (4 counts) ½ oz. triple sec (2 counts) 3 oz. sweet and sour (3 counts)	**SINGAPORE SLING-HIGHBALL OR DAIQUIRI** ½ oz. cherry-flavored brandy (2 counts) 1 oz. gin (4 counts) 2 oz. sweet and sour (2 counts) 1 oz. soda (1 count)
INCREDIBLE HULK-BUCKET 2 oz. cognac (8 counts) 2 oz. hypnotic ice (8 counts) **FRENCH 75** 1 oz. cognac (4 counts) 1 oz. lemon juice (1 count) dash of sugar (1 tsp.) splash of Champagne	**THUG'S PASSION-BUCKET** 2 oz. cognac (8 counts) 2 oz. Alize (8 counts)

scotch

SCOTCH	SCOTCH-SCOTCH-SCOTCH WHO'S GOT TWO THUMBS AND LOVES ... SCOTCH?
GODFATHER SNIFTER 1½ oz. Scotch (6 counts) ¾ oz. amaretto (3 counts)	**RUSTY NAIL BUCKET** 1½ oz. Scotch (6 counts) ¾ oz. Drambuie (3 counts)
ROB ROY MARTINI 2 oz. Scotch (8 counts) 1 oz. sweet vermouth (4 counts)	

VODKA	A BEAUTIFUL GIFT FROM OUR COMRADS
ADIOS MOTHER FUCKER/ ELECTRIC ICE TEA-DAIQUIRI ½ oz. vodka (2 counts) ½ oz. gin (2 counts) ½ oz. light rum (2 counts) ½ oz. blue Curacao (2 counts) 3 oz. sweet and sour (3 counts) splash of Sprite	**LONG ISLAND TEA-DAIQUIRI** ½ oz. vodka (2 counts) ½ oz. gin (2 counts) ½ oz. light rum (2 counts) ½ oz. tequila (2 counts) 3 oz. lemon juice (12 counts) splash of Coke
LONG ISLAND ICE TEA-DAIQUIRI ½ oz. vodka (2 counts) ½ oz. gin (2 counts) ½ oz. light rum (2 counts) ½ oz. tequila (2 counts) ½ oz. triple sec (2 counts) 2.5 oz. sweet and sour (2.5 counts) splash of Coke	**SHORT ISLAND ICE TEA-DAIQUIRI** ½ oz. vodka (2 counts) ½ oz. gin (2 counts) ½ oz. light rum (2 counts) ½ oz. triple sec (2 counts) 3 oz. sweet and sour (3 counts) splash of Coke

TEXAS TEA-DOWN-SIZED RECIPE-DAIQUIRI	TEXAS TEA-REGULAR SIZE RECIPE-PITCHER
½ oz. vodka (2 counts) ½ oz. gin (2 counts) ½ oz. light rum (2 counts) ½ oz. tequila (2 counts) ½ oz. triple sec (2 counts) ½ oz. bourbon (2 counts) 1 oz. sweet and sour (1 count) 1 oz. Coke (1 count)	2 oz. vodka (8 counts) 2 oz. gin (8 counts) 2 oz. light rum (8 counts) 2 oz. tequila (8 counts) 2 oz. triple sec (8 counts) 2 oz. bourbon (8 counts) 2 oz. sweet and sour (2 counts) 3 oz. Coke (3 counts)
LONG BEACH ICE TEA-DAIQUIRI	**TOKYO ICE TEA-DAIQUIRI**
½ oz. vodka (2 counts) ½ oz. gin (2 counts) ½ oz. light rum (2 counts) ½ oz. triple sec (2 counts) 3 oz. cranberry juice (3 counts) splash of sprite	½ oz. vodka (2 counts) ½ oz. gin (2 counts) ½ oz. light rum (2 counts) ½ oz. Midori (2 counts) 3 oz. sweet and sour (3 counts) splash of Sprite
GRATEFUL DEAD/PASSION TEA-DAIQUIRI	**VODKA COLLINS-HIGHBALL**
½ oz. vodka (2 counts) ½ oz. gin (2 counts) ½ oz. light rum (2 counts) ½ oz. crème de cassis (2 counts) 3 oz. sweet and sour (3 counts) splash of Sprite	1 oz. vodka (4 counts) 3 oz. sweet and sour (3 counts) splash of soda
GIMLET, VODKA-MARTINI	**MOSCOW MULE-HIGHBALL**
1½ oz. vodka (6 counts) 1½ oz. lime (6 counts)	1 oz. vodka (4 counts) ½ oz. lime (2 counts) 3 counts ginger ale
GIBSON-MARTINI	**MARTINI-MARTINI**
3 oz. vodka (12 counts) splash of dry vermouth (1 count) onion garnish	3 oz. vodka (or gin) (12 counts) splash of dry vermouth (1 count)
007 MARTINI- MARTINI	**FRENCH MARTINI-MARTINI**
1½ oz. premium vodka (6 counts) 1½ oz. premium gin (6 counts)	½ oz. Stoli vanilla vodka (2 counts) 1 oz. crème de cassis (4 counts) 3 oz. pineapple juice (3 counts)

APPLE MARTINI-MARTINI 1 ½ oz. vodka (6 counts) 1 ½ oz. Apple Pucker (6 counts)	**KEY LIME MARTINI-MARTINI** 1 oz. Stoli vanilla vodka (4 counts) 1 oz. lime juice (4 counts) 1 oz. pineapple juice (1 count) Splash of milk
MELON MARTINI-MARTINI 1 ½ oz. vodka (6 counts) 1 ½ oz. Melon Pucker (6 counts)	**CHOCOLATE** **MARTINI- MARTINI** ½ oz. Stoli vanilla vodka (2 counts) ½ oz. light crème de cacao (2 counts) ½ oz. Kahlua (2 counts) ½ oz. Baileys (2 counts) 2 oz. milk (2 counts) dash of chocolate
CHOCOLATE ESPRESSO **MARTINI-MARTINI-RAW** **SUGARED RIM** ½ oz. Stoli vanilla vodka (2 counts) ½ oz. light crème de cacao (2 counts) ½ oz. Kahlua (2 counts) ½ oz. Baileys (2 counts) 2 oz. milk (2 counts) dash of chocolate shot of espresso	**ESPRESSO** **MARTINI-MARTINI-RAW** **SUGARED RIM** 1½ oz. Stoli vanilla vodka (6 counts) ½ oz. crème de cacao (light) (2 counts) 1 oz. Kahlua (4 counts) shot of espresso
MACHETE-HIGHBALL 1 oz. vodka (4 counts) 4 oz. pineapple juice (4 counts)	**SCREW DRIVER-HIGHBALL** 1 oz. vodka (4 counts) 4 oz. orange juice (4 counts)
HARVEY **WALLBANGER-HIGHBALL** 1 oz. vodka (4 counts) 3 oz. orange juice (3 counts) 1 oz. float of Galliano (4 count)	**SLOW COMFORTABLE** **SCREW-HIGHBALL** ½ oz. vodka (2 counts) ¾ oz. Southern Comfort (3 counts) ¾ oz. sloe gin (3 counts) 3 oz. orange juice (3 counts)

SLOW COMFORTABLE SCREW AGAINST A WALL-HIGHBALL ½ oz. vodka (2 counts) ½ oz. Southern Comfort (2 counts) ¾ oz. sloe gin (3 counts) 3 oz. orange juice (3 counts) 1 oz. float of Galliano (4 count)	**QUICK FUCK-SHOT** 1/3 oz. vodka (1 count) 1/3 oz. Midori (1 count) 1/3 oz. Baileys (1 count)
PEARL HARBOR-HIGHBALL 1 oz. vodka (4 counts) ½ oz. Midori (2 counts) 4 oz. pineapple juice (4 counts)	**MELON BALL-HIGHBALL** 1 oz. vodka (4 counts) 1 oz. Midori (4 counts) 1½ oz. pineapple juice (1½ counts) 1½ oz. orange juice (1½ counts)
GREYHOUND-HIGHBALL 1 oz. vodka (4 counts) 4 oz. grapefruit juice (4 counts)	**SALTY DOG-HIGHBALL-SALTED RIM** 1 oz. vodka (4 counts) 4 oz. grapefruit juice (4 counts) 1 salted rim
RUSSIAN QUAALUDE-BUCKET ½ oz. vodka (2 counts) ½ oz. Malibu (2 counts) ½ oz. Frangelico (2 counts) 3 oz. milk (3 counts)	**BLACK RUSSIAN-BUCKET** 1 oz. vodka (4 counts) 3/4 oz. Kahlua (3 counts)
WHITE RUSSIAN-BUCKET 1 oz. vodka (4 counts) 3/4 oz. Kahlua (3 counts) Splash of milk	**COLORADO BULLDOG/.357 / SMITH &WESSON-BUCKET** 1 oz. vodka (4 counts) 1 oz. Kahlua (4 counts) 1½ counts milk 1½ oz. Coke (1½ counts)
CAPE COD-HIGHBALL 1 oz. vodka (4 counts) 4 oz. cranberry (4 counts)	**BAY BREEZE-HIGHBALL** 1 oz. vodka (4 counts) 1½ oz. cranberry (1½ counts) 1½ oz pineapple (1½ counts)
SEA BREEZE-HIGHBALL 1 oz. vodka (4 counts) 1½ oz. cranberry (1½ counts) 1½ oz. grapefruit juice (1½ counts)	**MADRAS-HIGHBALL** 1 oz. vodka (4 counts) 1½ oz. cranberry (1½ counts) 1½ oz. orange juice (1½ counts)

GOD MOTHER-SNIFTER 1½ oz. vodka (6 counts) ¾ oz. amaretto (3 counts)	**SILK PANTIES-SMALL** **BUCKET** ½ oz. vodka (2 counts) ½ oz. peach schnapps (2 counts)
HAIRY NAVEL-HIGHBALL 1 oz. vodka (4 counts) ½ oz. peach schnapps (2 counts) 3 oz. orange juice (3 counts)	**BON JOVI/WOO WOO/** **PIERCED NAVEL-HIGHBALL** 1 oz. vodka (4 counts) ½ oz. peach schnapps (2 counts) 3 oz. cranberry juice (3 counts)
SEX ON THE **BEACH-DAIQUIRI** 1 oz. vodka (4 counts) ½ oz. peach schnapps (2 counts) 1½ oz. cranberry juice (1½ counts) 1½ oz. pineapple juice (1½ counts)	**KAMIKAZE-BUCKET** 1 oz. vodka (4 counts) ½ oz. triple sec (2 counts) ¼ oz. lime (2 counts)
COSMOPOLITAN-MARTINI 1 oz. vodka (4 counts) ½ oz. triple sec (2 counts) ½ oz. lime (3 counts) splash of cranberry (1 count)	**WINDEX-BUCKET** 1¼ oz. vodka (5 counts) ¾ oz. blue Curacao (3 counts)
BLUE HAWAII-DAIQUIRI 1 oz. vodka (4 counts) ½ oz. blue Curacao (2 counts) 1 oz. coconut syrup (1 count) 3 oz. pineapple juice (3 counts)	**CHI CHI-DAIQUIRI** 1 oz. vodka (4 counts) 1 oz. coconut syrup (1 count) 1½ oz. milk (1½ counts) 1½ oz. pineapple juice (1½ counts)
LEMON **DROP-MARTINI-SUGARED** **RIM** 1½ oz. citron vodka (6 counts) ½ oz. triple sec (2 counts) 1 lemon (juiced) or 2 oz. lemon juice 2 tsp. of sugar	**PINK LEMONADE-MARTINI** 1 oz. citron vodka (4 counts) ½ oz. crème de cassis (2 counts) 3 oz. lemonade (3 counts) Use sweet and sour if lemonade is not available.
57 CHEVY-HIGHBALL ½ oz. vodka (3 counts) 1½ oz. Southern Comfort (6 counts) ½ oz. Grand Marnier (3 counts) 3 oz. pineapple juice (3 counts)	**LIQUID COCAINE-HIGHBALL** ½ oz. vodka (2 counts) ½ oz. Southern Comfort (2 counts) ½ oz. amaretto (2 counts) ½ oz. Grand Marnier (2 counts) 3 oz. pineapple juice (3 counts)

PURPLE HOOTER-BUCKET	PURPLE HAZE-BUCKET
1½ oz. citron vodka (6 counts)	1 oz. citron vodka (4 counts)
½ oz. triple sec (2 counts)	1 oz. crème de cassis (4 counts)
½ oz. crème de cassis (2 counts)	½ oz. sweet and sour (½ count)
	½ oz. Sprite (½ count)
BLOODY	**CAESAR-DAIQUIRI**
MARY-DAIQUIRI-SALTED RIM	1 oz. vodka (4 counts)
1 oz. vodka (4 counts)	4 oz. Clamato juice (4 counts)
3 drops Tabasco (or a drop of	
horseradish—½ tsp.)	
2 drops steak sauce (½ tsp.)	
dash of pepper	
dash of salt, dash of celery salt	
3 oz. tomato juice (3 counts)	
SCREAMING	**NUTS AND BERRIES-BUCKET**
ORGASM-BUCKET	½ oz. crème de cassis (2 counts)
½ oz. vodka (2 counts)	½ oz. Baileys (2 counts)
½ oz. amaretto (2 counts)	½ oz. Frangelico (2 counts)
½ oz. Baileys (2 counts)	3 oz. milk (3 counts)
½ oz. Kahlua (2 counts)	
3 oz. milk (3 counts)	

GIN	AHH … LIKE SIPPING ON A PINE TREE
MARTINI-MARTINI 3 oz. gin (12 counts) splash of dry vermouth (use only ¼ oz.)	**GIMLET, GIN-MARTINI** 1½ oz. gin (6 counts) 1½ oz. lime (6 counts)
GIN LIME-MARTINI 1½ oz. gin (6 counts) 1½ oz. lime (6 counts)	**GIN TONIC-HIGHBALL** 1 oz. gin (4 counts) 4 oz. tonic (4 counts)
TOM COLLINS-HIGHBALL 1 oz. gin (4 counts) 3 oz. sweet and sour (3 counts) 1 oz. soda (1 count)	**GIN FIZZ-HIGHBALL** 1 oz. gin (4 counts) 3 oz. sweet and sour (3 counts) 1 oz. soda (1 count) (egg white optional)
GIN RICKEY-HIGHBALL 1 oz. gin (4 counts) ½ oz. lime juice (2 counts) 3 oz. soda (3 counts)	**GIN BUCK-HIGHBALL** 1 oz. gin (4 counts) ½ oz. lemon juice (2 counts) 3 oz. ginger ale (3 counts)
FLYING DUTCHMAN-MARTINI 3 oz. gin (12 counts) ½ oz. triple sec (2 counts)	**NEGRONI-MARTINI** 1 oz. gin (4 counts) 1 oz. sweet vermouth (4 counts) 1 oz. Campari (4 counts)

RUM	FREAKY ISLAND STYLE WITHOUT THE RUM? NO WAY MAN!
DAIQUIRI-DAIQUIRI 1½ oz. light rum (6 counts) 1½ oz. lime juice (6 counts) dash of simple syrup (1 tsp.) scoop of ice, blended	**FLAVORED DAIQUIRIS-DAIQUIRI** 1 oz. light rum (4 counts) ½ oz. lime juice (2 counts) ½ oz. drop of simple sugar (2 count) 3 oz. fruit juice (3 counts) of the flavor you desire
PIÑA COLADA-DAIQUIRI 1 oz. light rum (4 counts) 1 oz. coconut syrup (1 count) 1½ oz. milk (1½ counts) 1½ oz. pineapple juice (1½ counts)	**LAVA FLOW-DAIQUIRI** 1 oz. light rum (4 counts) ½ oz. crème de banana (2 counts) (or half a real banana) 1½ oz. milk (1½ counts) 1½ oz. pineapple juice (1½ counts) Swirl the glass with strawberry syrup.
BAHAMA MAMA-DAIQUIRI ½ oz. coconut rum (2 counts) ¼ oz. 151 rum (1 count) ¼ oz. Kahlua (1 count) 3 oz. pine apple juice (3 counts) 2 lemon wedges 1 oz. float of dark rum (4 counts)	**BACARDI COCKTAIL-MARTINI** 1 oz. Bacardi light rum (4 counts) ¼ oz. lime juice (2 counts) ½ lime, squeezed splash of grenadine (1 count)

CABLE CAR-MARTINI Sugar rimmed 2 oz. vanilla-flavored rum (8 counts) ½ oz. orange Curacao (2 counts) ½ oz. lime juice (2 counts) or ½ lime, squeezed 1 oz. sweet and sour (1 count) dash of cinnamon on top	**OLD FASHION MAI TAI-BUCKET** 2 oz. light rum (8 counts) ½ oz. orange Curacao (2 counts) ½ oz. orgeat syrup (½ count) ¼ oz. simple syrup (a dash) juice from whole lime
MAI TAI-DAIQUIRI 1 oz. light rum (4 counts) ½ oz. triple sec (2 counts) ½ oz. orgeat syrup (1/2 count) 1½ oz. pineapple juice (1½ counts) 1½ oz. orange juice (1½ counts) Juice from 1 lime and 1 lemon wedge 1 oz. float of dark rum (4 counts)	**ZOMBIE-HURRICANE** 1 oz. light rum (4 counts) ½ oz. triple sec (2 counts) ½ oz. orgeat syrup (1/2 count) 1½ oz. pineapple juice (1½ counts) 1½ oz. orange juice (1½ counts) juice from 1 lime and 1 lemon wedge ½ oz. float each of dark rum (2 counts) and 151 rum (2 counts)
PLANTER'S PUNCH-DAIQUIRI 1 oz. light rum (4 counts) ½ oz. triple sec 2 counts) ½ oz. orgeat syrup (1/2 count) 1½ oz. pineapple juice (1½ counts) 1½ oz. orange juice (1½ counts) juice from 1 lime and 1 lemon wedge ½ oz. float of dark rum (2 counts) squirt of grenadine (1 count)	**MOJITO-DAIQUIRI** 3 oz. light rum (12 counts) 2 lime wedges (squeezed and put in) 2 pinches of sugar (2 tsp.) 2–4 mint sprigs 1 oz. soda (1 count)
SCORPION-DAIQUIRI 1 oz. light rum (4 counts) 1 oz. brandy (4 counts) 1½ oz. orange juice (1½ counts) juice from 1 lime wedge pinch of sugar (1 tsp.) 1 oz. float of dark rum (4 counts)	**RUM RUNNER-DAIQUIRI** 1 oz. coconut rum (4 counts) 1 oz. blackberry brandy (4 counts) 1 oz. orange juice (1 count) 1 oz. pineapple juice (1 count) 1 oz. cranberry juice (1 count)

JAMAICAN QUAALUDE-BUCKET	RED ROOSTER-DAIQUIRI
½ oz. coconut rum (2 counts) ½ oz. Frangelico (2 counts) ½ oz. Baileys (2 counts) 3 oz. milk (3 counts)	1½ oz. 151 rum (6 counts) ½ oz. crème de noyaux (2 counts) 3 oz. guava juice (3 counts) splash of grenadine (1 count)
XYZ-MARTINI 2 oz. rum (8 counts) ¾ oz. triple sec (3 counts) ¾ oz. lemon juice (6 counts)	

TEQUILA

TEQUILA NOT JUST FOR THE WORMS	
ORIGINAL STYLE MARGARITA-MARGARITA/ MARTINI 1 ½ oz. premium tequila (6 counts) ½ oz. Cointreau (2 counts) 2 oz. lime (2 counts) or half of a fresh lime 1 oz. float of Grand Marnier (6 counts)	**MARGARITA-MARGARITA** 1 ½ oz. tequila (6 counts) ½ oz. triple sec (2 counts) 2 oz. lime (2 counts) 3 oz. sweet and sour (3 counts)
BLUE MARGARITAS-MARGARITA 1 ½ oz. tequila (6 counts) 2 oz. lime (2 counts) 1/2 oz. blue Curacao (2 counts) 3 oz. sweet and sour (3 counts)	**GREEN MARGARITAS-MARGARITA** 1 ½ oz. tequila (6 counts) 1 oz. Midori (4 counts) 3 oz. sweet and sour (3 counts)

FLAVORED MARGARITA-MARGARITA 1 ½ oz. tequila (6 counts) ½ oz. triple sec (2 counts) 3 oz. flavored syrup or fresh fruit (3 counts) 1 oz. drop of simple sugar (1 count) (if needed)	**ULTIMATE MARGARITA-MARGARITA** 1 ½ oz. premium tequila (6 counts) 1/2 oz. Cointreau (2 counts) 3 oz. lime (2 counts) 3 oz. sweet and sour (3 counts)
ITALIAN MARGARITA-MARGARITA 1 oz. tequila (4 counts) ½ oz. amaretto (2 counts) 3 oz. sweet and sour (3 counts)	**CADILLAC MARGARITA-MARGARITA** 1 ½ oz. premium tequila (6 counts) 1/2 oz. Cointreau (2 counts) 1/2 oz. lime (2 counts) 3 oz. sweet and sour (3 counts) float of Grand Marnier (4 counts)
TEQUILA SUNRISE- DAIQUIRI 1 oz. tequila (4 counts) 4 oz. orange juice (4 counts) squirt of grenadine (1 count)	**PINK CADILLAC-MARGARITA** 1 1/2 oz. premium silver tequila (6 counts) 1/2 oz. lime (2 counts) 1 oz. cranberry juice (1 count) 2 oz. sweet and sour (2 counts) 1 oz. float of Grand Marnier (4 counts)

CORDIALS & LIQUORS	Who Doesn't Love The Sweet Stuff?
APPLE PIE-MARTINI 2 oz. apple schnapps (8 counts) 1 oz. cinnamon schnapps (4 counts)	**FRENCH CONNECTION-SNIFTER** 1½ oz. cognac (6 counts) ¾ oz. amaretto (3 counts)
SMITH AND KEARNS-BUCKET 1 oz. Kahlua (4 counts) 2 oz. milk (2 counts) 1 oz. soda (1 count)	**TOASTED ALMOND- BUCKET** 1 oz. Kahlua (4 counts) ¾ oz. amaretto (3 counts) 2 oz. milk (2 counts)
CHOCOLATE STRAWBERRY-MARTINI 1 ½ oz. strawberry schnapps (6 counts) 1 oz. white crème de cacao (4 counts) 2 dashes chocolate (2 tsp.) (2 counts) splash of milk (½ count)	**WHITE CHOCOLATE STRAWBERRY-MARTINI** 1 oz. strawberry schnapps (4 counts) 1 oz. white crème de cacao (4 counts) ½ oz. Baileys (2 counts) splash of milk (½ count)

GOLDEN CADILLAC-DAIQUIRI-BLENDED 2 oz. light crème de cacao (8 count) 3 oz. milk (3 counts) blended with 1 oz. float of Galliano (4 counts)	**GRASSHOPPER-DAIQUIRI-BLENDED** ¾ oz. green crème de menthe (3 counts) ¾ oz. light crème de cacao (3 counts) 3 oz. milk (3 counts)
ITALIAN DRIVER/AMARETTO AND OJ-HIGHBALL 1 oz. amaretto (4 counts) 4 oz. orange juice (4 counts)	**FUZZY NAVEL-HIGHBALL** 1½ oz. peach schnapps (6 counts) 3 oz. orange juice (3 counts)
SURFER ON ACID-BUCKET 1 oz. Jagermeister (4 counts) 1 oz. coconut rum (4 counts) 2 oz. pineapple juice (2 counts)	**ITALIAN SURFER-BUCKET** 1 oz. amaretto (4 counts) 1 oz. coconut rum (4 counts) 2 oz. pineapple juice (2 counts)
SEXY MOTHER FUCKER-BUCKET ¾ oz. amaretto (3 counts) ¼ oz. Southern Comfort (1 count) ¼ oz. lime (1 count) 3 oz. cranberry juice (3 counts)	**ITALIAN SURFER ON ACID-BUCKET** ½ oz. amaretto (2 counts) ½ oz. coconut rum (2 counts) ½ oz. Jagermeister (2 counts) 2 oz. pineapple juice (2 count)
QUAALUDE-BUCKET 1 oz. Frangelico (4 counts) 1 oz. Baileys (4 counts) 3 oz. milk (3 counts)	**ALABAMA SLAMMER-HIGHBALL** 1 oz. amaretto (4 counts) 1 oz. Southern Comfort (4 counts) ½ oz. slow gin (2 counts) 3 oz. orange juice (3 counts)
JAMAICAN QUAALUDE-BUCKET ½ oz. Malibu (2 counts) ½ oz. Frangelico (2 counts) ½ oz. Baileys (2 counts) 3 oz. milk (3 counts)	**RUSSIANQUAALUDE-BUCKET** ½ oz. vodka (2 counts) ½ oz. Frangelico (2 counts) ½ oz. Baileys (2 counts) 3 oz. milk (3 counts)

ROOT BEER-BEER MUG 1 oz. Kahlua (4 counts) 3 oz. soda water (3 counts) 1 float of Galliano (4 counts)	**MONKEY FUCK-HIGHBALL** ½ oz. vodka (2 counts) ½ oz. crème de banana (2 counts) ½ oz. Baileys (2 counts) 3 oz. milk (3 counts)
ORGASM-BUCKET ½ oz. amaretto (2 counts) ½ oz. Baileys (2 counts) ½ oz. Kahlua (2 counts) 3 oz. milk (3 counts)	**ROOT BEER FLOAT-BEER MUG** 1 oz. Kahlua (4 counts) 1½ oz. milk (1½ counts) 1½ oz. soda water (1½ counts) 1 float of Galliano (4 counts)
SEXY ALLIGATOR-MARTINI IN THIS ORDER 1 oz. crème de cassis (4 counts) 1 oz. Midori (4 counts) (shaken) 1 oz. Jagermeister float (4 Counts)	**SCREAMING ORGASM-BUCKET** ½ oz. vodka (2 counts) ½ oz. amaretto (2 counts) ½ oz. Baileys (2 counts) ½ oz. Kahlua (2 counts) 3 oz. milk (3 counts)

SHOTS
SHOTS!
THE WORD ITSELF CREATES EXCITEMENT! MANY WONDERFUL SHOT DRINKS EXIST— BLOW JOBS, BUTTERY NIPPLES, SCREAMING ORGASMS, COCK-SUCKING COWBOYS … JUST ABOUT SOMETHING FOR EVERYONE!

SHOT; ADJECTIVE: WOVEN AS TO PRESENT A PLAY OF COLORS.

SHOT; VERB: AN AIMED STOKE, THROW, OR THE LIKE, AS IN CERTAIN GAMES, ESPECIALLY IN AN ATTEMPT TO SCORE.

SHOT; NOUN: A SMALL QUANTITY, ESPECIALLY AN OUNCE OF UNDILUTED LIQUOR.

ONE-OUNCE SHOTS	
GORILLA FART-SHOT GLASS ½ oz. wild turkey (2 counts) ½ oz. 151 rum (2 counts)	**SCREAMING NAZI-SHOT** ½ oz. Jagermeister (2 counts) ½ oz. Rumplemintz (2 counts)
BUTTERY ASS-SHOT GLASS ½ oz. Jagermeister (2 counts) ½ oz. butterscotch schnapps (2 counts)	**BUTTERY NIPPLE-SHOT GLASS** ½ oz. Baileys (2 counts) ½ oz. butterscotch schnapps (2 counts)
SLIPPERY NIPPLE-SHOT GLASS ½ oz. Baileys (2 counts) ½ oz. Sambuca (2 counts)	**CHINA WHITE-SHOT GLASS** ½ oz. Baileys (2 counts) ½ oz. crème de cacao (2 counts) sprinkle of cinnamon
IRISH GOLD-SHOT GLASS ½ oz. Baileys (2 counts) ½ oz. Goldschlager (2 counts)	**BRAIN HEMORRHAGE-SHOT GLASS** ½ oz. Baileys (2 counts) ½ oz. peach schnapps (2 counts) small squirt of grenadine
SILK PANTIES-SHOT GLASS ½ oz. vodka (2 counts) ½ oz. peach schnapps (2 counts)	**OLD DIRTY BASTARD-SHOT GLASS** ½ oz. amaretto (2 counts) ½ oz. crown royal (2 counts) small squirt of chocolate
SICILIAN KISS-SHOT GLASS ½ oz. amaretto (2 counts) ½ oz. Southern Comfort (2 counts)	**POPPER-SHOT GLASS** ½ oz. tequila (2 counts) ½ oz. Sprite (½ count)

DUCK FART-SHOT GLASS 1/3 oz. Kahlua (1½ counts) 1/3 oz. Baileys (1½ counts) 1/3 oz. Canadian Whiskey (1½ counts)	747-SHOT GLASS 1/3 oz. Kahlua (1½ counts) 1/3 oz. Baileys (1½ counts) 1/3 oz. Frangelico (1½ counts)
B-52-SHOT GLASS 1/3 oz. Kahlua (1½ counts) 1/3 oz. Baileys (1½ counts) 1/3 oz. Grand Marnier (1½ counts)	BLOW JOB-SHOT GLASS IF YOU USE YOUR HANDS TO DRINK, THIS SHOT IS CALLED A **HAND JOB** 1/3 oz. Kahlua (1½ counts) 1/3 oz. Baileys (1½ counts) crème de banana (1½ counts) topped with whipped cream (add a cherry on top and it's called a **Muff Diver**)
COCK-SUCKING COWBOY-SHOT GLASS 1/3 oz. Kahlua (1½ counts) 1/3 oz. Baileys (1½ counts) crème de banana (1½ counts).	BLACK DEATH-SHOT GLASS 1/3 oz. Kahlua (1½ counts) 1/3 oz. Baileys (1½ counts) 1/3 oz. black Sambuca (1½ counts)
TIGER'S EYE-SHOT GLASS 1/3 oz. Kahlua (1½ counts) 1/3 oz. Rumplemintz (1½ counts) 1/3 oz. Jagermeister (1½ counts)	PB AND J-SHOT GLASS 1/3 oz. Frangelico (1½ counts) 1/3 oz. vodka (1½ counts) 1/3 oz. crème de cassis (1½ counts)
WINDEX-SHOT GLASS 1/3 oz. vodka (1½ counts) 1/3 oz. triple sec (1½ counts) 1/3 oz. blue Curacao (1½ counts)	QUICK FUCK-SHOT GLASS 1/3 oz. vodka (1½ counts) 1/3 oz. Baileys (1½ counts) 1/3 oz. Midori (1½ counts)
JELLYFISH-SHOT GLASS 1/3 oz. white crème de cacao (1½ counts) 1/3 oz. Baileys (1½ counts) 1/3 oz. amaretto (1½ counts) squirt of grenadine, layered	

ONE-OUNCE JUICY SHOTS	
WET PUSSY-BUCKET ½ oz. vodka (2 counts) ½ oz. Apple Pucker (2 counts) 1 count cranberry juice	**PINK LEMONADE-BUCKET** ½ oz. citron vodka (2 counts) ½ oz. crème de cassis (2 counts) 1 oz. lemonade (1 count)
MIND ERASER-BUCKET ½ oz. vodka (2 counts) ½ oz. Kahlua (2 counts) 3 oz. soda water (3 counts) **ON THE ROCKS AND DRUNK** **FROM A STRAW. YES, THAT'S** **RIGHT, IT'S A SHOT . . .**	**PIECE OF ASS-BUCKET** ¾ oz. amaretto (3 counts) ¼ Southern Comfort (1 count) ½ oz. lime (2 counts)
NUTTY IRISHMAN-BUCKET ½ oz. Baileys (2 counts) ½ oz. Frangelico (2 counts) splash of milk (1½ counts)	**CEMENT MIXER-2 SHOT** **GLASSES** 1 oz. Baileys (4 counts) 1 oz. lime juice (6 count) **TWO SHOTS IN THE** **MOUTH, THE SUBJECT'S** **HEAD IS SHAKEN, AND THE** **CONCOCTION IS DRUNK** **DOWN.**

IRISH CAR BOMB-SHOT GLASS ½ oz. Baileys (2 counts) ½ oz. Irish whiskey (2 counts) dropped into one Guinness beer	**ROOSTER TAIL-3 SHOT GLASSES** 1 oz. tequila (4 counts) 1 oz. orange juice (1 count) 1 oz. tomato juice (1 count)
SAKE BOMBS-SHOT GLASS 1 oz. sake dropped into one draft beer	**BOILER MAKER/DEPTH CHARGE-SHOT GLASS** 1 oz. shot of whiskey dropped into one draft beer
DR. PEPPER-SHOT GLASS ¾ oz. amaretto (3 counts) ¼ 151 rum (1 count) (light with fire) dropped into a draft beer glass half full of beer and half full of Coke	**JAGER BOMBS-SHOT GLASS** 1 oz. Jager dropped into one glass half filled with any energy drink
YELLOW CAKE-BUCKET 1/3 oz. vanilla vodka (1½ counts) 1/3 oz. triple sec (1½ counts) 1/3 oz. pineapple juice	**NUTS AND BERRIES-BUCKET** 1/3 oz. Frangelico (1½ counts) 1/3 oz. Baileys (1½ counts) 1/3 oz. crème de cassis (1½ counts) dash of milk (1 count)

OVER-ONE-OUNCE SHOTS	DO YOU GET THE PICTURE? A TWO-OUNCE SHOT OF JACK IS A REALLY BIG SHOT TO BE SLAMMING DOWN. A ONE-OUNCE SHOT OF CHIVAS IN A BUCKET OR A ONE-OUNCE SHOT OF FRANGELICO IN A SNIFTER IS AN AWFULLY LONELY SHOT.
GORGEOUS 1 oz. Cognac (4 counts) 1 oz. Grand Marnier (4 counts) 1 oz. amaretto (4 counts)	**BEAUTIFUL** 1 oz. Cognac (4 counts) 1 oz. Grand Marnier (4 counts)
CHIVAS NEAT/NAKED 1 glass (bucket) 2 oz. scotch	**FRENCH CONNECTION** 1 oz. Cognac (4 counts) 1 oz. amaretto (4 counts)

PURPLE HOOTER-BUCKET	POUSSE CAFÉ-PONY OR
1½ oz. citron vodka (6 counts) ½ oz. triple sec (2 counts) ½ oz. crème de cassis (2 counts)	SHORT FLUTE Equal parts: grenadine, 1/4 oz. (1 count) chartreuse (yellow), 1/4 oz. (1 count) crème de cassis, 1/4 oz. (1 count) cream de menthe (white), 1/4 oz. (1 count) chartreuse (green), 1/4 oz. (1 count) brandy, ¼ oz. (1 count)
THREE WISE MEN ½ oz. Johnny Walker (2 counts) ½ oz. Jim Bean (2 counts) ½ oz. Jack Daniels (2 counts) PUT THIS ONE IN A BUCKET AS THIS IS A MAN'S DRINK—A FOOLISH MAN—BUT THAT'S BESIDE THE POINT.	

OVER ONE-OUNCE JUICY SHOTS	SHOTS LIKE THESE YOU PUT IN A SMALL BUCKET OR MARTINI GLASSES. ONCE IN THE MARTINI GLASS THEY BECOME MARTINIS AND THE PARTY MIGHT START TO MOVE A BIT.
KAMAKAZI-BUCKET 1 oz. vodka (4 counts) ½ oz. triple sec (2 counts) ¼ oz. lime (2 counts)	THE KAMIKAZE CAN BE MADE IN MANY DIFFERENT COLORS—BLUE (USE BLUE CURACAO INSTEAD OF TRIPLE SEC); GREEN (USE MIDORI INSTEAD OF TRIPLE SEC); PINK (USE CRÈME DE CASSIS INSTEAD OF TRIPLE SEC.)
LEMON DROP-BUCKET SUGARED RIM 1 oz. citron vodka (4 counts) ½ oz. triple sec (2 counts) juice from 1 lemon or 1 ½ oz. lemon juice dash of sugar (1 tsp.)	**PURPLE HAZE-BUCKET** 1 oz. citron vodka(4 counts) 1 oz. crème de cassis (4 counts) ½ oz. sweet and sour (½ count) ½ oz. soda (½ count)
CHOCOLATE CAKE-BUCKET-SUGARED RIM 1 oz. citron vodka (4 counts) 1 oz. Frangelico (4 counts) shaken, sugar rim, garnished with a sugar-coated lemon wedge	**MELLON BALL-BUCKET** 1 oz. vodka (4 counts) ½ oz. Midori (2 counts) 1 oz. orange juice (1 count) 1 oz. pineapple juice (1 count)

PINK SQUIRREL-BUCKET 1 oz. light crème de cacao (4 counts) ½ oz. cream de noyaux (2 counts) (Use ½ oz. Frangelico and a splash of grenadine if you don't have the noyaux.) 1 oz. splash of milk (1 count)	**JOLLY RANCHER-BUCKET** 1 oz. vodka (4 counts) ½ oz. Midori (2 counts) 1½ oz. cranberry juice (1½ counts)
SWEET TIGHT PUSSY-BUCKET 1 oz. peach schnapps (4 counts) ½ oz. Midori (2 counts) 1½ oz. pineapple juice (1½ counts) ½ oz. splash of Sprite (½ count)	**SCOOBY SNACK-BUCKET** ½ oz. Malibu (2 counts) ½ oz. Midori (2 counts) 1 oz. pineapple juice (1 count) splash of cream, shaken
THROW ME DOWN AND FUCK ME-BUCKET 1/3 oz. vodka (1½ counts) 1/3 oz. Malibu (1½ counts) 1/3 oz. peach schnapps (1½ counts) 1 oz. pineapple juice (1 count) 1 oz. orange juice (1 count)	**MORNING HEAD-BUCKET** 1/3 oz. vanilla vodka (1½ counts) 1/3 oz. Cointreau (1½ counts) 1/3 oz. Midori (1½ counts) ½ oz. splash of grenadine (1 count) 2 oz. orange juice (2 counts)
RED-HEADED SLUT-BUCKET 1 oz. peach schnapps (4 counts) 1½ oz. cranberry juice (1½ count) 1 oz. Jagermeister (4 counts) (float)	**ORGASM-BUCKET** 1/3 oz. Baileys (1½ counts) 1/3 oz. Kahlua (1½ counts) 1/3 oz. amaretto (1½ counts) 1 oz. splash of milk (1 count)
SCREAMING ORGASM-BUCKET ¼ oz. vodka (1 count) ¼ oz. Baileys (1 count) ¼ oz. Kahlua (1 counts) ¼ oz. amaretto (1 count) 1 oz. splash of milk (1 count)	**ITALIAN SURFER-BUCKET** 1 oz. amaretto (4 counts) 1 oz. coconut rum (4 counts) 2 oz. pineapple juice (2 counts)

SURFER ON ACID-BUCKET 1 oz. Jagermeister (4 counts) 1 oz. coconut rum (4 counts) 2 oz. pineapple juice (2 counts) **OATMEAL COOKIES-BUCKET** ¼ oz. Jagermeister (1 count), ¼ oz. Goldschlager (1 count) ¼ oz. butterscotch schnapps (1 count) ¼ oz. Baileys (1 count) splash of cream	**ITALIAN SURFER ON ACID-BUCKET** ¾ oz. amaretto (3 counts) ¾ oz. coconut rum (3 counts) ¾ oz. Jagermeister (3 counts) 2 oz. pineapple juice (2 counts)

BLENDED DRINKS ... NOTHING'S BETTER	AT A PARTY, WOULD YOU HIDE YOUR BEST FRIEND IN THE CLOSET? THE BLENDER IS YOUR FRIEND; DON'T HIDE HIM AND ACT LIKE HE'S NOT AROUND.
MARGARITA-MARGARITA 1½ oz. tequila (6 counts) ½ oz. triple sec (2 counts) ¼ oz. lime (2 counts) 3 oz. sweet and sour (3 counts) **ITALIAN MARGARITA-MARGARITA** 1 oz. tequila (4 counts) ½ oz. amaretto (2 counts) 3 oz. sweet and sour (3 counts) **PIÑA COLADA-DAIQUIRI** 1 oz. light rum (4 counts) 1 oz. coconut syrup (1 count) 1½ oz. milk (1½ counts) 1½ oz. pineapple juice (1½ counts)	DAIQUIRI WILL ALWAYS HAVE RUM; ONLY THE JUICE WILL CHANGE. I RECOMMEND THREE OUNCES OF FLAVORED SYRUP OR FRESH FRUIT WITH FLAVORED DAIQUIRIS. FOR EXAMPLE: PEACH, MANGO, PASSION FRUIT, PINEAPPLE, STRAWBERRY, BANANA ... TIP: DEPENDING ON THE FRESHNESS OF THE FRUIT, DAIQUIRIS MIGHT NEED MORE OR LESS SUGAR ADDED TO THEM.

LAVA FLOW-DAIQUIRI
1 oz. light rum (4 counts)
½ oz. crème de banana (2 counts)
(or half a real banana)
1½ oz. milk (1½ counts)
1½ oz. pineapple juice (1½ counts)
Swirl the glass with strawberry
syrup before you pour the drink.

CHOCOLATE
MONKEY-DAIQUIRI
½ oz. dark crème de cacao (2
counts)
½ oz. crème de banana (2 counts)
3 oz. milk (3 counts)
1 oz. squirt of chocolate (1 count)

STRAWBERRY
SHORTCAKE-DAIQUIRI
1 oz. amaretto (4 counts)
½ oz. light crème de cacao (2
counts)
1 oz. strawberry syrup (1 count)
3 oz. milk (3 counts)
Swirl this glass with strawberry
syrup and graham cracker rim.

GOLDEN CADILLAC-
DAIQUIRI-BLENDED
2 oz. light crème de cacao (8
counts)
3 oz. milk (3 counts) blended
1 oz. float of Galliano (4 counts)

DAIQUIRI-DAIQUIRI
1½ oz. light rum (6 counts)
1½ oz. lime juice (6 counts)
dash of simple syrup (1 tsp.)
scoop of ice, blended

ITALIAN/NUTTY
COLADA-DAIQUIRI
1 oz. amaretto (4 counts)
1 oz. coconut syrup (1 count)
1½ oz. milk (1½ counts)
1½ oz. pineapple juice (1½ counts)

CHI CHI-DAIQUIRI
1 oz. vodka (4 counts)
1 oz. coconut syrup (1 count)
1½ oz. milk (1½ counts)
1½ oz. pineapple juice (1½ counts)

MUDSLIDE-DAIQUIRI
½ oz. vodka (2 counts)
1 oz. Kahlua (4 counts)
½ oz. Baileys (2 counts)
3 oz. milk (3 counts)
½ oz. squirt of chocolate (½ count)
(optional)
Swirl the glass with chocolate.

FLAVORED
DAIQUIRIS-DAIQUIRI
1½ oz. light rum (6 counts)
½ oz. lime juice (2 counts)
1 oz. drop of simple sugar (1 count)
3 oz. the fruit juice (3 counts) of
any flavor you desire

CHAMPAGNE & WINE	SUNDAY MONRNINGS AND PARTIES THAT START WITH A POP; WHO DOES THEM BETTER THEN CHAMPAGNE
MIMOSA-FLUTE 4 oz. Champagne (4 counts) splash of fresh orange juice (1 count)	THERE ARE A MILLION AND A HALF RECIPES FOR SANGRIA. I GIVE YOU THREE QUICK AND EASY WAYS TO MAKE IT WITH YOUR CHOICE OF EITHER THE EXPENSIVE OR THE COST-EFFECTIVE WAY. MAKE THEM COLD AND CUSTOMERS WILL LOVE THEM BOTH WAYS.

BELLINI-FLUTE 4 oz. Champagne (4 counts) splash of peach puree (1 count) **SCORPINI-FLUTE** 2 oz. Champagne (2count) ½ oz. vodka (2 counts) 3 scoops of lemon sorbet splash of limoncello (1 count), blended Garnish with crushed coffee beans.	**RED SANGRIA-WINE GLASS** 3 oz. red wine (3 counts) ½ oz. brandy (2 counts) ½ oz. Chambord (2 counts) 2 oz. Champagne (2 counts) 1 oz. sugar (1 count) fresh fruit (apples, strawberries, blue berries, grapes, oranges, raspberries … best to use what is in season) **POOR MAN'S RED** **SANGRIA-WINE GLASS** 3 oz. red wine (3 count) 1 oz. gin (4 counts) ½ oz. grenadine (4 counts) (lemons and cherries) splash of Sprite **WHITE SANGRIA** 3 oz. white wine (3count) ½ oz. cognac (2 counts) ½ oz. peach schnapps (2 counts) 2 oz. Champagne (2 counts) 1 oz. sugar (1 count) fresh fruit (apples, strawberries, peaches, Champagne grapes, pears, oranges, lychee, red raspberries … best to use what is in season)

FRENCH 75-SNIFTER 1 oz. cognac (4 counts) 1 oz. lemon juice (1 count) dash of sugar (1 tsp.) top with Champagne	SPRITZER-WINE GLASS 3 oz. white wine (3 counts) splash of soda (1 count)
KIR ROYALE-FLUTE 4 oz. Champagne (4 count) splash of cassis (1 count) . . . just a little!	KIR-WINE GLASS 4 oz. white wine (4count) ¼ oz. cassis (1 count)
	WINE COOLER-WINE GLASS 3 oz. white wine (3 count) splash of Sprite (1 count)

BEER DRINKS	WHO SAID BEER DRINKERS CAN'T HAVE A FEW FANCY DRINKS? WE MIX IT UP SOMETIMES TOO!
DR. PEPPER-SHOT AND PINT ¾ oz. amaretto (3 counts) ¼ oz. 151 rum (1 count) Light rum on fire and drop into ½ of beer and ½ Coke in rocks glass. **RED EYE/ RED ROOSTER-PINT** ¾ draft beer ¼ tomato or Bloody Mary mix	**BOILER MAKER/DEPTH CHARGE-PINT** 1 oz. shot of whiskey (4 counts) Drop into one draft beer. **JAGER BOMBS-SHOT AND PINT** 1 oz. Jagermeister (4 counts) Drop into glass half filled with any energy drink

CARIBBEAN NIGHT-PINT
1 oz. Kahlua (4 counts)
1 draft beer

SNAKE BITE-PINT
½ beer (usually stout)
½ cider

BLACK VELVET-PINT
½ beer (usually stout)
½ Champagne

HANGOVER MEDICINE-PINT
½ draft beer
½ tomato or Bloody Mary mix
1 raw egg
a few drops of hot sauce

SAKE BOMBS-PINT
1 oz. sake (4 counts)
Drop into a draft beer.

IRISH CAR BOMB-SHOT AND PINT
½ oz. Baileys (2 counts)
½ oz. Irish whiskey (2 counts)
Drop into a Guinness beer.

HOT DRINKS ... SOMETHING NICE TO SNUGGLE DOWN WITH ON THE COLD NIGHTS

IRISH COFFEE-COFFEE GLASS 1 oz. Baileys (4 counts) 1 oz. Irish whiskey (4 counts) 3 counts of coffee	**ITALIAN COFFEE-COFFEE GLASS** 1 oz. Baileys (4 counts) 1 oz. amaretto (4 counts) 3 counts of coffee
CHIP SHOT-COFFEE GLASS 1 oz. Baileys (4 counts) 1 oz. Tuanka (4 counts) 3 counts of coffee	**MEXICAN COFFEE-COFFEE GLASS** 1 oz. Kahlua (4 counts) 1 oz. tequila (4 counts) 3 counts of coffee
KEOKI COFFEE/SPANISH COFFEE-COFFEE GLASS 1 oz. Kahlua (4 counts) 1 oz. brandy (4 counts) 3 counts of coffee	**RUSSIAN COFFEE-COFFEE GLASS** 1 oz. vodka (4 counts) 1 oz. Frangelico (4 counts) 3 counts of coffee

JAMAICAN COFFEE-COFFEE GLASS 1 oz. rum (4 counts) 1 oz. Tia Maria (4 counts) 3 counts of coffee	TENNESSEE MUD-COFFEE GLASS 1 oz. whiskey (4 counts) 1 oz. amaretto (4 counts) 3 counts of coffee
HOT TODDY-COFFEE GLASS 1 oz. whiskey (4 counts) dash of honey 2 counts of hot water 1 oz. lemon juice 1 slice of lemon	

VIRGIN DRINKS	IF YOU'RE TRYING TO GET YOUR GOOD TIMES ON WITHOUT THE GOOD STUFF, HERE ARE A FEW CLASSIC RECIPES
VIRGIN DAIQUIRI 3 oz. desired flavor (sweet and sour for regular) 2 oz. lime juice (8 counts) 1 scoop of ice, blended	**ICE CREAM PUNCH-BOWL** Cranberry juice, orange juice, pineapple juice, Sprite (all equal parts) 1 scoop of vanilla ice cream
SHIRLEY TEMPLE/KIDDY COCKTAIL 1 Sprite squirt of grenadine (1 count)	**ROY ROGERS** Coke and a squirt of grenadine (1 count)
ROOT BEER FLOAT/BLACK COW 1½ oz. root beer (1½ counts) 2 scoops of vanilla ice cream	**VIRGIN CHI CHI/PIÑA COLADA** 1 oz. coconut syrup (1 count) 1½ oz. milk (1½ counts) 1½ oz. pineapple juice (1½ counts) 1 scoop of ice

SHAKE Ice cream (3 large scoops) 2 oz. milk (2 counts)	**VIRGIN MARGARITA** 2 oz. sweet and sour (2 counts) 2 oz. lime juice (2 counts) 1 oz. orange juice (1 count) 1 scoop of ice, blended
CREAMSICLE 1½ oz. orange juice (1½ counts) 2 scoops of vanilla ice cream (blended)	**ORANGE JULIUS** 1½ oz. orange juice (2 counts) 1½ oz. milk (2 counts) 1 scoop ice (blended)
LEMONADE 1 whole lemon squeezed or 1½ oz. lemon juice 4 tsp. of sugar 3 oz. water (3 counts) Shake and pour over ice.	**LEMON SQUASH** 1 whole lemon squeezed or 1½ oz. lemon juice 1½ oz. sugar syrup (1½ counts) 3 oz. soda (3 counts)

WHAT DRINKS
BUILD ON EACH OTHER?

Vodka Gimlets
Vodka + Lime
6 counts 6 counts
Kamikazes
Vodka + Triple Sec + Lime
4 counts, 2 counts, 2 counts
Cosmos
Vodka + Triple Sec + Lime + Cranberry
4 counts, 2 counts, 2 counts, 1 count

Vodka Martinis
Vodka
12 counts
Vodka Gimlets
Vodka + Lime
6 counts, 6 counts
Moscow Mules
Vodka + Lime + Ginger Ale
4 counts, 2 counts, 3 counts

Black Russians
Vodka + Kahlua
4 counts, 3 counts
White Russians
Vodka + Kahlua + Milk
4 counts, 3 counts, 1 count
Colorado Bulldogs/.357/Smith and Wesson
Vodka + Kahlua + Milk + Coke
4 counts, 3 counts, 1 count, 1 count

Silk Panties
Vodka + Peach Schnapps
2 counts, 2 counts
Bon Jovi/Woo Woos/Pierced Navels
Vodka + Peach Schnapps + Cranberry Juice
4 counts, 2 counts, 3 counts
Sex on the Beaches
Vodka + Peach Schnapps + Cranberry Juice + Pineapple Juice
 4 counts, 2 counts, 1½ counts, 1½ counts

Vodka Martinis
Vodka
12 counts
Apple Martinis
Vodka + Apple Pucker
6 counts, 6 counts
Wet Pussys
Vodka + Apple Pucker + Cranberry Juice
2 counts, 2 counts, 1 count

Gin Martinis
Gin
12 counts
Gin Gimlets
Gin + Lime
6 counts, 6 counts
Gin Rickeys
Gin + Lime + Soda
4 counts, 2 count, 3 counts

Cricket
White crème de cacao, white crème de menthe, splash of cream
4 counts, 2 count, 1½ counts

Locust
White crème de cacao, white crème de menthe, 151 rum, and splash of cream
4 counts, 2 counts, 2 counts, 1 count

Virgin Bloody Mary
Bloody Mary mix
5 counts
Red Eyes
Beer + Bloody Mary Mix
4 counts, 1 count
Hangover Medicines
Beer + Bloody Mary Mix + 1 Raw Egg + Hot Sauce
 2 counts, 3 counts
Mai Tais
Light Rum + Triple Sec + Orgeat Syrup + Pineapple Juice + Orange Juice + Lemon Juice +
4 counts,   2 counts,   .5 count,   1½ counts,   1½ counts
1 count
Lime Juice + a Float of Dark Rum
1 count,   4 counts,

Planters Punch
Light Rum + Triple Sec + Orgeat Syrup + Pineapple
4 counts,   2 counts,   .5 count,   1½ counts
Juice + Orange Juice + Lemon Juice + Lime Juice + grenadine + a Float of Dark Rum
1½ counts,   1 count,   1 count,   2 counts,   4 counts

Zombie

Light Rum + Triple Sec + Orgeat Syrup + Pineapple
4 counts,   2 counts,   .5 counts,   1½ counts
Juice + Orange Juice + Lemon Juice + Lime Juice + Float of Dark
Rum + Float of 151rum
1½ counts,   1 count,   1 count,   2 counts,   2 counts

WHAT DRINKS ARE SIMILAR?

COMPARISON CHARTS

BRANDY ALEXANDER	SUBSTITUTE	PINK SQUIRREL
Brown Crème de Cacao ½ oz. (2 counts) **Brandy 1 oz. (4 counts)** Milk (1½ counts)	➜	White Crème de Cacao ½ oz. (2 counts) **Crème de Noyaux 1 oz. (4 counts)** Milk (1½ counts)

GOLDEN CADILLAC	SUBSTITUTE	GRASSHOPPER
White Crème de Cacao 2 oz. (8 counts) **Galliano 1 oz. (4 counts)** Milk (1½ counts)	➜	White Crème de Cacao 1 oz. (4 counts) **Green Crème de Menthe ½ oz. (2 counts)** Milk (1½ counts)

GRASSHOPPER	SUBSTITUTE	CRICKET
White Crème de Cacao 1 oz. (4 counts) **Crème de Menthe ½ oz. (2 counts)** Milk (1½ counts)	➜	Crème de Cacao 1 oz. (4 counts) **White Crème de Menthe ½ oz. (2 counts)** Milk (1½ counts)

GODMOTHERS	SUBSTITUTE	GODFATHERS
Amaretto ¾ oz. (3 counts) **Vodka 1½ oz. (6 counts)**	➜	Amaretto ¾ oz. (3 counts) **Scotch 1½ oz. (6 counts)**

SCREWDRIVER	ADD	HARVEY WALLBANGER
Vodka 1 oz. (4 counts) Orange Juice (4 counts)	➜	Vodka 1 oz. (4 counts) Orange Juice (3 counts) **Galliano 1 oz. (4 counts)**

PEARL HARBOR	ADD	MELON BALL
Vodka 1 oz. (4 counts) Midori ½ oz. (2 counts) Pineapple juice (3 counts)	→	Vodka 1 oz. (4 counts) Midori ½ oz. (2 counts) Pineapple juice (1½ counts) **Orange Juice (1½ counts)**

BAY BREEZE	SUBSTITUTE	SEA BREEZE	MADRAS
Vodka 1 oz. (4 counts) Cranberry Juice (2 counts) **Pineapple Juice (2 counts)**	→	Vodka 1 oz. (4 counts) Cranberry Juice (2 counts) **Grapefruit Juice (2 counts)**	Vodka 1 oz. (4 counts) Cranberry Juice (2 counts **Orange Juice (2 counts**

KAMIKAZE	SUBSTITUTE	WINDEX
Vodka 1 oz. (4 counts) **Triple Sec ½ oz. (2 counts)** Lime (2 counts)	→	Vodka 1 oz. (4 counts) **Blue Curacao ½ oz. (2 count)** Lime (2 counts)

CHI CHI	SUBSTITUTE	PIÑA COLADA
Vodka 1 oz. (4 counts) Coconut Syrup (1 count) Pineapple Juice (1½ counts) Milk (1½ counts)	→	**Rum 1 oz. (4 counts)** Coconut Syrup (1 count) Pineapple Juice (1½ counts) Milk (1½ counts)

57 CHEVY	ADD	LIQUID COCAINE
Vodka ½ oz. (2 counts) Southern Comfort 1 ½ oz. (6 counts) Grand Marnier ½ oz. (2 counts) Pineapple Juice (3 counts)	→	Vodka ½ oz. (2 counts) Southern Comfort ½ oz. (2 counts) Grand Marnier ½ oz. (2 counts) **Amaretto ½ oz. (2 counts)** Pineapple Juice (3 counts)

ORGASM	ADD	SCREAMING ORGASM
Amaretto ½ oz. (2 counts) Baileys ½ oz. (2 counts) Kahlua ½ oz. (2 counts) Milk (1 count)	+	**Vodka ½ oz. (2 count)** Amaretto ½ oz. (2 counts) Baileys ½ oz. (2 counts) Kahlua ½ oz. (2 counts) Milk (1 count)

LEMON DROP	ADD	PINK LEMONADE
Citron Vodka 1½ oz. (6 counts) Triple Sec ½ oz. (2 counts) Sweet and Sour (3 counts) Simple sugar ½ oz. (2 counts)	+	Citron Vodka 1½ oz. (6 counts) Triple Sec ½ oz. (2 counts) Sweet and Sour (3 counts) Simple sugar ½ oz. (2 counts) **splash of cranberry (1 count)**

GIMLET	EQUALS	GIN LIME
Gin 1½ oz. (6 counts) Lime Juice 1½ oz. (6 counts)	=	Gin 1½ oz. (6 counts) Lime Juice 1½ oz. (6 counts)

RUM & COKE	ADD	CUBA LIBRE
Rum 1 oz. (4 counts) Coke (4 counts)	+	Rum 1 oz. (4 counts) Code (4 counts) **Lime slice**

MAI TAI	SUBSTITUTE	ZOMBIE
Light Rum 1 oz. (4 counts) Triple Sec ½ oz. (2 counts) Orgeat Syrup (½ count) Pineapple Juice (1½ counts) Orange Juice (1½ counts) Lemon Juice (1 count) Lime Juice (1 count) 1 oz. float of Dark Rum (4 counts)	→	Light Rum 1 oz. (4 counts) Triple Sec ½ oz. (2 counts) Orgeat Syrup (½ count) Pineapple Juice (1½ counts) Orange Juice (1½ counts) Lemon Juice (1 count) Lime Juice (1 count) **½ oz. float of Dark Rum (2 counts)** **½ oz. float of 151 Rum (2 counts)**

QUAALUDE	ADD	RUSSIAN QUAALUDE	SUBSTITUTE	JAMACIAN QUAALUDE
Frangelico 1 oz. (4 counts) Baileys 1 oz. (1 count) Milk (1½ counts)	✛	**Vodka ½ oz. (2 counts)** Frangelico 1 oz. (4 counts) Baileys 1 oz. (4 counts) Milk (1½ counts)	➔	**Malibu ½ oz. (2 counts)** Frangelico 1 oz. (4 counts) Baileys 1 oz. (4 counts) Milk (1½ counts)

(This chart is all 2 counts.)

DUCK FART	747	B52	COCK-SUCKING COWBOY	BLOW JOB	BLACK DEATH	SUBSTITUTE ADD
Kahlua + Baileys +	Kahlua + Baileys +	Kahlua + Baileys +	Kahlua + Baileys +	Kahlua + Baileys +	Kahlua + Baileys +	
Rye Whiskey	Frangelico	Grand Marnier	Crème de Banana	Crème de Banana/ whipped crème (garnish with a cherry and it's called a Muff diver)	Sambuca	

BUTTERY NIPPLE	ADD	OATMEAL COOKIE
Baileys ½ oz. (2 counts) Butterscotch Schnapps ½ oz. (2 counts)	✛	Baileys ¼ oz. (1 count) Butterscotch Schnapps ¼ oz. (1 count) **Jagermeister ¼ oz. (1 count)** **Goldschlager ¼ oz. (1 count)** **Splash of cream**

SICILIAN KISSES	ADD	PIECES OF ASS	SEXY MOTHERFUCKERS
Amaretto ½ oz. (2 counts) Southern Comfort ½ oz. (2 counts)	✛	Amaretto ¾ oz. (3 counts) Southern Comfort ½ oz. (2 counts) **Lime Juice (2 counts)**	Amaretto ¾ oz. (3 counts) Southern Comfort ¼ (1 count) Lime Juice (2 counts) **Cranberry Juice (3 counts)**

ITALIAN SURFERS	SUBSTITUTE/ ADD	SURFERS ON ACID	ITALIAN SURFERS ON ACID
Amaretto 1 oz. (4 counts) Coconut Rum 1 oz. (4 counts) Pineapple (2 counts)	➜✛	**Jagermeister 1 oz. (4 counts)** Coconut rum 1 oz. (4 counts) Pineapple (2 counts)	**Amaretto ¾ oz. (3 counts)** **Jagermeister ¾ oz. (3 counts)** Coconut rum ¾ oz. (3 counts) Pineapple (2 counts)

FUZZY NAVEL	ADD	HAIRY NAVEL
Peach Schnapps 1½ oz. (6 counts) Orange Juice (3 counts)	✛	**Vodka 1 oz. (4 counts)** Peach Schnapps 1/2 oz. (2 counts) Orange Juice (3 counts)

MARGARITA	SUBSTITUTE	LYNCHBURG LEMONADE	SIDECAR

Tequila 1 oz. (4 counts) Triple Sec ½ oz. (2 counts) Sweet and Sour (3 counts) Lime (2 counts)	→	Whiskey 1 oz. (4 counts) Triple Sec ½ oz. (2 counts) Sweet and Sour (3 counts)	Cognac 1 oz. (4 counts) Triple Sec ½ oz. (2 counts) Sweet and Sour (3 counts)

BARTENDING TESTS

Training a new bartender?
Need to determine a bartender's skill level?

Test 1
What's the difference between a Gibson and a gimlet?

What two drinks change their names because of their garnish?

What three things do you ask when someone orders a martini?

What three things do you ask when someone orders a margarita?

Someone orders a vodka tonic. Name three vodkas you could recommend to them in order to up sell.

Someone orders a gin tonic. Name three gins you could recommend to them in order to up sell.

What is the order in which you make drinks?

1. Glass
2.
3.
4. Juice
5.

Place these liquors in the order in which they should be poured: Rye, Vodka, Gin, Bourbon, Tequila, Brandy, Rum, Scotch, Triple sec

Do you make blended drinks first or last?

Place these drinks in the order in which they should be made: Margarita, Vodka Tonic, Tom Collins, Mojito, Tequila Sunrise

What is a Black Russian with milk and Coke called?

What is a gin lime with ginger ale called?

What's the difference between a mai tai and a zombie?

What's the difference between an apple martini and a Washington apple martini?

What's the difference between an apple martini and a wet pussy?

How do you make a Cape Codder, a sea breeze, and a bay breeze?

What is in a sex on the beach?

What is in a screwdriver? A machete?

What's the difference between a hairy navel and a fuzzy navel?

What's the difference between a piña colada and a chi chi?

Test 2

When building a drink order, in what order do the following items go?
Ice, Juice, Liquor, Glass, Soda

When you're building your drinks do you start from the left and go right or from the right and go left?

Do your ever cross your hands?

Place these drinks in the order in which they should be made:
Gin Tonic, Tequila Sunrise, Vodka Collins, Daiquiri, Coke

If you were making a piña colada and a vodka Collins which one would you make first?

Name four drinks that are similar or build off of each other.
1._____and a_____ 2._____and a_____
3._____and a_____ 4._____and a_____

When layering a shot, in which order would you add Kahlua, Baileys, and crème de banana?

What is the name of this shot?_____ and if you put whipped cream on it?_____ whipped cream and a cherry?_____

What is the difference between bourbon and whiskey?

What is the difference between Champagne and sparkling white wine?

Provide two examples where the garnish is so important that it changes the name of a drink.

What do these terms mean?
Perfect
Neat
Up

Straight Up

On average about how much liquor and juice are in each of the following drinks?
Vodka martini:_____Screwdriver:_____Cosmopolitan:_____
Shot of Jack Daniels:_____ Grand Marnier in a snifter:_____

You walk into the bar you see that the bar is not restocked. What are the first five things that you do to prep the bar and make sure you are ready to go?

Name two rye whiskeys:

Name two Irish whiskeys:

Name two bourbons:

Name one brandy:

Name two Scotches:

Name two single-malt Scotches:

In the next few questions name one well brand and one top-shelf brand.
Name two vodkas:

Name two gins:

Name three rums (light, gold, and dark):

Name two tequilas:

What is a vodka lime with ginger ale called?

Test 3
Fill in the blanks

Cocktail Name	Glass	Liquor oz.	Juice oz.	Soda oz.
Golden Cadillac				
Grasshopper				
Bay Breeze				
Sea Breeze				
Madras				
Tequila Sunrise				
Piña Colada				
Chi Chi				
Lava Flow				
57 Chevy				
Liquid cocaine				
Orgasm				
Lemon drop				
French martini				
Beautiful				
French connection				
Manhattan				
Quaalude				
Jamaican Quaalude				
Duck fart				

747				
B-52				
Cock-sucking cowboy				
Blow job				
Buttery nipple				
Slippery nipple				
Surfer on acid				
Fuzzy navel				
Hairy navel				
Margarita				
Lynchburg lemonade				
Side car				
Cuba Libre				

Example Inventory List

PRODUCT INVENTORY			IN BAR	RESTOCK	IN STORAGE	ORDER
Date						
CO2 level						
RYE WHISKEY						
CANADIAN CLUB						
CROWN ROYAL						
SEAGRAM'S 7						
SEAGRAM'S VO						
WHISKEY						
JACK DANIELS						
GENTLEMAN JACK						
JIM BEAM						
WILD TURKEY						
WILD TURKEY 101						
WILD TURKEY RARE BREED						
MAKERS MARK						
IRISH WHISKEY						
JAMESON						
BUSHMILL						
BRANDY						

JAQUES CARDIN						
CHRISTIAN BROS						
COUVOISIER VS						
COUVOISIER VSOP						
HENNESSY VS						
HENNESSY VSOP						
MARTELL CORDON BLUE						
MARTELL VS						
MARTELL VSOP						
MEXTAXA 7 STAR						
REMY VS						
REMY VSOP						
REMY XO						
SCOTCH						
CLUNY						
J&B						
DEWERS						
DEWERS 12YR						
CUTTY SARK						
ABERLOUR 10YR						
BALLANTINES						
BALVENIE 10YR						
BALVENIE 12YR DBL WOOD						
BALVENIE 15YR						
CHIVAS REGAL						
CHIVAS REGAL 18YR						
GLENFIDDICH						

GLENLIVET 12YR						
GLENLIVET 18YR						
GLENMORANGIE 10YR						
GLENMORANGIE 18YR						
JOHNNY WALKER BLK LABEL						
JOHNNY WALKER RED LABEL						
MACALLAN 12YR						
MACALLAN 18YR						
WOODFORD RESERVE						
VODKA						
SEAGRAM'S						
ABSOLUT						
ABSOLUT CITRON						
ABSOLUT KURANT						
ABSOLUT MANDARIN						
ABSOLUT PEPPER						
BELVEDERE						
GREY GOOSE						
CHOPIN						
FINDLANDIA						
KETTLE ONE						
KETTLE ONE CITRON						

SKYY						
SKYY CITRUS						
SKYY BERRY						
SKYY VANILLA						
SKYY MELON						
SKYY ORANGE						
SKYY SPICED						
STOLICHNAYA						
STOLI ORANGE						
STOLI RASPBERRY						
STOLI VANILLA						
HANGAR ONE						
VAN GOGH						
GIN						
SEAGRAM'S						
BEEFEATER						
BOMBAY						
BOMBAY SAPPHIRE						
TANQUERAY						
TANQUERAY TEN						
HENDRICK'S						
BOODLES						
BAFFERTS						
RUM						
BACARDI SILVER						
BACARDI 151						
LEMON HART						
BACARDI COCO						
BACARDI GOLD						

BACARDI LEMON						
BACARDI ORANGE						
BACARDI CICLON						
CAPTAIN MORGAN						
MALIBU						
MOUNT GAY						
MYER'S DARK						
TEQUILA						
MONTEZUMA						
ALMENDRADO						
CAZADORES REPOSADO						
TRES GENERATIONS						
CUERVO GOLD						
CUERVO 1800						
HERRADURA ANJEO						
SAUZA						
PATRON SILVER						
PATRON GOLD						
CORDIALS						
AMARETTO BOLS						
AMARETTO DISARANO						
AMARETTO DISARANO TALEA						
ANISETTE						
APPLE PUCKER SCHNAPPS						

APRICOT BRANDY BOLS						
B&B						
BAILEYS						
BLACKBERRY BRANDY						
BLUE CURACAO BOLS						
BORGHETTI						
BUTTERSHOTS						
CHAMBORD						
CHARTREUSE						
CHERRY BRANDY						
COINTREAU						
CRÈME DE BANANA						
CRÈME DE CASSIS BOLS						
CRÈME DE CACAO DARK BOLS						
CRÈME DE CACAO LIGHT BOLS						
CRÈME DE MENTHE GREEN BOLS						
CRÈME DE MENTHE WHITE BOLS						
CRÈME DE NOYAUX BOLS						
DRAMBUIE						
FRANGELICO						
GALLIANO						
GOLDSCHLAGER						
GRAND MARNIER						

IRISH MIST						
JAGERMEISTER						
JUST DESSERT CHO CHIP COOKIE						
KAHLUA						
LIMONCELLO						
LIMONCELLO CREAM						
MIDORI						
MONTENEGO						
ORANGE CURACAO						
OUZO						
PEACH BRANDY						
PEACH SCHNAPPS BOLS						
PEPPERMINT SCHNAPPS						
PERNOD						
ROOT BEER						
SAMBUCA GENERIC						
SAMBUCA LIGHT						
SAMBUCA DARK						
SLOE GIN BOLS						
SOUTHERN COMFORT						
STRAWBERRY						
TIA MARIA						
TRIPLE SEC BOLS						
WATERMELON PUCKER						

APERITIFS					
AVERNA					
CAMPARI					
CYNAR					
DUBONNET ROUGE					
FERNET BRANCA					
LILLET BLOND					
MARTINI&ROSSI BIANCO					
MARTINI&ROSSI DRY					
MARTINI&ROSSI SWEET					
NOILLY PRAT DRY					
PIMMS					
PUNT Y MES					
GRAPPA					
CHIARLO GAVI					
CHIARLO BAROLO					
SASSICIA					
CANDOLINI RUTA					
CANDOLINI BIANCA					
TIGNANELLO, ANTINORI					
SAPRA, JACOPO POLI					
WHITE WINE					

PINOT GRIGIO						
PINOT BLANCO						
CHARDONNAY						
WHITE ZIN						
SPARKING WINE						
CHAMPAGNE						
RED WINE						
PINOT NOIR						
CHIANTI						
MERLOT						
CABERNET						
SYRAH						
RED ZIN						
BEER						
BUD						
BUD LIGHT						
MGD						
MILLER LIGHT						
AMSTEL LIGHT						
COORS LIGHT						
BECKS						
HEINEKEN						
MORETTI						
MORETTI RED						
GUINNESS						
BASS						
CORONA						
HACK BECK						

SHARPS						
WATER						
SPARKLING						
FLAT						
SODAS						
SPRITE						
COKE						
DIET						
GINGER ALE						
TONIC						
CRANBERRY						
LEMONADE						
COFFEE SUPPLIES						
ESPRESSO PACKS						
DECAF ESPRESSO PACKS						
COFFEE						
DECAF COFFEE						
FILTERS						
JUICES, MIXES, AND SYRUPS						
LIME JUICE						
GRENADINE						
SWEET AND SOUR						

BLOODY MARY MIX						
STRAWBERRY MIX						
MANGO MIX						
PIÑA COLADA MIX						
BANANA MIX						
PEACH PUREE						
PASSION MIX						
PINEAPPLE JUICE						
GRAPEFRUIT JUICE						
TOMATO JUICE						
CRANBERRY JUICE						
RED BULL						
SIMPLE SYRUP						
ORGEAT SYRUP						
CHOCOLATE SYRUP						
STRAWBERRY SYRUP						
GARNISHES						
LEMONS						
LIMES						
CHERRIES						
OLIVES						
BLUE CHEESE OLIVES						
PICKLED ONIONS						
FRESH MINT						
ORANGES						
STRAWBERRIES						

APPLES						
PINEAPPLE						
BANANAS						
CUCUMBER						
CELERY						
CONDIMENTS						
TABASCO SAUCE						
STEAK SAUCE						
HORSERADISH						
BLACK PEPPER						
SALT (COARSE)						
SUGAR						
POWDERED SUGAR						
BITTERS						
CINNAMON						
NUTMEG						
MILK						
CREAM						
WHIPPED CREAM						
BAR ITEMS						
LARGE STRAWS						
SMALL STRAWS						
PLASTIC TOOTHPICKS						
NAPKINS						
GARBAGE BAGS						
POURERS						
WINE KEYS						

PENS						
TIN						
GLASS TUMBLER						
STRAINER						
LONG MAT						
RECTANGULAR MAT						
JIGGERS						
GLASSWARE						
BUCKET						
SODA						
COLLIN/ HIGHBALL						
WINE						
BALLOON WINE						
MARTINI						
SNIFTER						
SHOT GLASS						
PONY GLASS						
BEER GLASS						
DAIQUIRI GLASS						
HURRICANE GLASS						
CHAMPAGNE GLASS						
COFFEE GLASS						
COFFEE CUP						
ESPRESSO CUP						

LAYERING CHART

Start with your heavier ingredients first—the **higher number**, the **heavier** the ingredients. Pour using the back of the spoon.

LIQUOR/LIQUID	GRAVITY/ DENSITY	COLOR
SOUTHERN COMFORT	0.97	LIGHT AMBER
TUACA	0.98	AMBER
WATER	1.00	WHITE/CLEAR
EN CHARTREUSE	1.01	GREEN
COINTREAU	1.04	WHITE
PEACH LIQUEUR	1.04	DARK AMBER
SLOE GIN	1.04	WHITE
KUMMEL	1.04	WHITE
PEPPERMINT SCHNAPPS	1.04	WHITE
BENEDICTINE	1.04	WHITE
BRANDY	1.04	AMBER
MIDORI	1.05	GREEN
APRICOT BRANDY	1.06	AMBER
BLACKBERRY BRANDY	1.06	DARK RED
CHERRY BRANDY	1.06	DARK RED
PEACH BRANDY	1.06	DARK AMBER
CAMPARI	1.06	RED
YELLOW CHARTREUSE	1.06	YELLOW
DRAMBUIE	1.08	WHITE/CLEAR
FRANGELICO	1.08	WHITE/CLEAR
ORANGE CURACAO	1.08	ORANGE
TRIPLE SEC	1.09	WHITE/CLEAR
TIA MARIA	1.09	BROWN

APRICOT LIQUEUR	1.09	AMBER
BLACKBERRY LIQUOR	1.10	DARK RED
AMARETTO	1.10	LIGHT BROWN
BLUE CURACAO	1.11	BLUE
CHERRY LIQUOR	1.12	DARK RED
GALLIANO	1.11	GOLDEN YELLOW
GREEN CRÈME DE MENTHE	1.12	GREEN
WHITE CRÈME DE MENTHE	1.12	WHITE
STRAWBERRY LIQUEUR	1.12	RED
PARFAIT D'AMOUR	1.13	VIOLET
COFFEE LIQUEUR	1.14	DARK BROWN
CRÈME DE BANANA	1.14	YELLOW
DARK CRÈME DE CACAO	1.14	BROWN
WHITE CRÈME DE CACAO	1.14	WHITE/CLEAR
KAHLUA	1.15	DARK BROWN
CRÈME DE ALMOND	1.16	LIGHT BROWN
CRÈME DE NOYAUX	1.17	BRIGHT RED
ANISETTE	1.17	WHITE/CLEAR
CRÈME DE CASSIS	1.18	PURPLE

MEASUREMENTS AND CALORIES

Squeezing the bottle

One 750 ml bottle should make 12 cocktails with 2 oz. of liquor (2 shots).
One 750 ml bottle should make 17 cocktails with 1.5 oz. of liquor (a shot and a half).
One 750 ml bottle should make 25 cocktails with 1 oz. of liquor (a shot).

One 750 ml bottle should make four to five glasses of wine per bottle. Use the "two fingers from the rim of the glass" rule, and you should always get four nice glasses of wine, depending on the size of the glass; 9 oz. and smaller is recommended.

750 ml = 25.5 oz.
500 ml = 17 oz.
200 ml = 6.8 oz.
1,000 ml = 34.1 oz.
1,750 ml = 59.7 oz.
1 liter = 33.8 oz.

1 teaspoon (tsp.) = 1/8 oz.
1 tablespoon (tbs.) = 3/8 oz.
1 glass of wine = 5 oz.
1 glass of Champagne = 6 oz.
1 pint (pt.) = 16 oz.
1 quart (qt.) = 32 oz.
1 gallon (gal.) = 128 oz.

Calories in Your Drinks

12 oz. beer = around 144 calories and up

12 oz. lite beer = around 125 and up

(The darker the beer and the higher the alcohol content the greater the calories.)

5 oz. red wine = around 95 calories

5 oz. white wine = 90 calories

6 oz. Champagne = 200 calories

(The sweeter the white wine the higher the calories.)

1 oz. shot = about 65 calories

2 oz. juicy shot (2 oz. of liquor and 2 oz. juice or soda) = about 153 calories

3 oz. martini = about 195 calories

5 oz. cocktail (1 oz. liquor and 4 oz. juice or soda) = around 112 calories and up

5 oz. cocktail (1 oz. liquor and 4 oz. milk) = around 215 calories and up

These figures are based on 80 proof liquor, soda and juice with 11.67 calories per ounce, and whole milk with 150 calories per serving (15 ml).

Mixers' Calorie Content

5 oz. Bloody Mary mix = 46

5 oz. pineapple juice = 132

5 oz. ginger ale = 62

6 oz. Sprite = 74

5 oz. orange juice = 75

5 oz. cranberry juice = 137

5 oz. lemonade = 395

5 oz. average energy drink = 110

5 oz. coffee = 2

5 oz. milk = 228

5 oz. soda water = 0

5 oz. of cola = 136

5 oz. of diet cola = 0

6 oz. tonic = 124

5 oz. eggnog = 343

(Taken from http://www.dietbites.com/calorieindexdrinks.html)

Web sites

Book Website
www.whosyourbartender.com

Drinking Stories
http://www.tuckermax.com/stories.phtml

Recipe Web Sites
www.webtender.com
www.acats.org
www.epicurious.com/drinking
www.cocktail.com/
www.cocktail-finder.com
www.droogle.ca
http://www.webtender.com
www.cocktailtimes.com
www.cocktaildb.com

Drinking Magazine Sites
www.moderndrunkardmagazine.com
www.esquire.com/foodanddrink/database/frame_main1.html
www.allaboutbeer.com
www.imbibemagazine.com
www.fineexpressions.co.uk
www.whiskymag.com
www.wineandspiritsmagazine.com
www.winemag.com/homepage/index.asp
www.alestreetnews.com
www.allaboutbeer.com
www.beeradvocate.com
www.wineontheweb.com
www.dailylush.com

Beer Clubs

www.worldbeerdirectory.com
www.amazingbeerclub.com
www.beeramerica.com
www.beermonthclub.com
www.microbeerclub.com
www.flyingnoodle.com/clubs_beer.html
www.worldofbrews.tripod.com
www.greatclubs.com/beerofthemonthclub
www.mrbeer.com
www.beermonthclubs.com

Wine

Wine Spectator www.winespectator.com
Wine-Wikipedia http://en.wikipedia.org/wiki/Wine
Wines.com www.wines.com
Food and Wine www.foodandwine.com/wine/
Damn Good Wine www.damngoodwine.com
Wine Families www.pfv.org/
Robert Parker and wine www.erobertparker.com
Wine topix www.winetopix.com
Sommnet www.sommnet.com
Ozclarke.com www.ozclarke.com
The wine show www.thewineshow.com
The origins of wine www.museum.upenn.edu
Wine brats www.winebrats.org
Wine lover's page www.wineloverspage.com
Wine Info net www.wineinfonet.com
Wine Release www.winereleasedate.com

Wine Stuff

Wine Enthusiast www.wineenthusiast.com
Calvines www.calvines.com
Drink stuff www.drinkstuff.com/products/wine-stuff.asp
Rosehill wine Cellars www.rosehillwinecellars.com
www.barfly.com

Uncorked www.uncork.com.
The Wine Rack shop www.winerackshop.com
Westside Wine Cellars http://westsidewinecellars.com
Wine Accessories www.wineaccessory.com
The Wine Rack store www.winerackstore.com
Wine Accessories wineracksplansandmore.com
Wine Wall www.wine-wall.com

Wine Making
International wine consultants www.wine-consultants.com
Winemaker www.iwinemaker.com
Winemaker home page http://winemaking.jackkeller.net
Homebrew shop www.homebrewshop.com/wine.html
Wonderwine www.wonderwine.com

Buying Wine
Wine searcher www.wine-searcher.com
The Wine Web www.wineweb.com
Wine Tours www.wine-tours.com
Wine shoppers www.wineshoponline.com
Burgundy Online http://burgundyonline.com
Dee vine wines www.dvw.com
Fine Wines International www.vinrare.com/home.jsp
Finest wines www.finestwine.com
Ice wine http://www.icewineniagara.net
Internet wine and spirits http://randalls.stores.yahoo.net/wines.html
Italian wine direct www.italianwinesdirect.com
Market wine and spirits www.marketfinewine.com/index.html
Organic wines http://www.organicwine.com.au/
Saratoga www.e-winegifts.com
The Wine Specialists http://www.winespecialist.com
Napa cabs www.wine-club-central.com
Vino World http://www.winoworld.com

Wine.com www.wine.com

Wine Auctions
Wine Auction www.winesellarauction.com
The Wine Commune www.winecommune.com

Wine Clubs
Californian wine club www.californiareds.com/
wine-of-the-month-club.html
Passport www.geerwade.com/WineClubHome.aspx
Amazing Wine Club www.amazingwineclub.com

Wine Organizations
Italian Sommelier Association www.aiscalifornia.com
North American Association of Sommeliers
www.nasommelier.com

DAVID WILLIAM VANCIL

On May 16, 1978, David William Vancil was born in Chicago, Illinois, where he spent his childhood years. Upon turning the age of eighteen he set off for the sands of the Hawaiian Islands, where he spent the next four years. Having arrived in Hawaii at a young age, David was not sure what direction he would take to launch a career. The beauty and elegance of the Royal Hawaiian Hotel located on Waikiki Beach brought about an opportunity where he took his first step toward becoming the ultimate bartender that he is today. Putting college on the back burner, David decided to turn up the heat and further pursue a career in bartending, later accepting a job at Scruples, also located on Waikiki Beach. Scruples was a place that had hot, sexy, animalistic energy, body shots, and bartenders who worked like machines.

The international waters called David's name in 1999 after one of his regular customers offered him a partnership opportunity to open a club in Japan. David found himself at the age of twenty-two with no money and a plane ticket to Japan. He hit the ground running and found a job working in Ryopungi at One-Eyed Jacks and Gas Panic, the latter a club of massive human contact. People were packed like sardines into this bar, with bartenders breathing fire and girls dancing on top of the bar wearing no panties! He then ventured off and started working at the Kagetsu Hotel in Isawa, Japan—a bar covered in marble with koi rivers running throughout private rooms along with hostesses, geisha, and yakuza!

On January 31, 2001, the time had come for David and his partner to open his first club, the Sexy Mother Fucker Club 69 in Kofu, Japan. After hard work and sacrifices David had reached a time in his life where at the age of twenty-five he questioned who he was and where his life was going. Reflecting on his time in Japan he realized that along with making good friends, having some great times, and dealing with stress and challenges, this was a time when he found his soul put to the test.

At this point in David's life all arrows led back to the United States. The first stop was Hollywood, where David began working at La Piazza in August of 2003, Lolas Martini bar, The Yard House, and Drai's at the W Hotel. Surrounded by ambitious people in the entertainment industry and many people "trying to get a break," David continues to seek future opportunities to make a difference in the lives of others. He has found enjoyment in everyday bartending while making lemons into lemonade, and you can too! This book is your chance to let David make a difference in your life and to become the ultimate bartender you've always dreamed you could be!